LIBRARY INSTRUCTION AND FACULTY DEVELOPMENT:

GROWTH OPPORTUNITIES IN THE ACADEMIC COMMUNITY

Papers Presented at the Twenty-Third Midwest
Academic Librarians' Conference held at
Ball State University, May 1978.

edited by
Nyal Z. Williams
and **Jack T. Tsukamoto**

Published by
Pierian Press
ANN ARBOR, MICHIGAN
1980

Library of Congress Catalog Card No. 80-82263
ISBN 0-87650-125-0

Copyright © 1980, The Pierian Press
All Rights Reserved

PIERIAN PRESS
P.O. Box 1808
Ann Arbor, Michigan 48106

Contents

Foreword . . . . page vii
    Ray R. Suput

Preface . . . . page ix
    The editors

Faculty Development in an Age of Uncertainty . . . . page 1
    Jesse McCartney

**Faculty Development from a Librarian's
Point of View** . . . . page 11
    Dwight F. Burlingame

**The Role of the Librarian in Faculty Development;
A Professor's Point of View** . . . . page 17
    Paul A. Lacey

**Library Instruction and Instructional
Development** . . . . page 29
    Patricia Senn Breivik

**Bibliographic Instruction at Earlham: A Cooperative
Course--Related Approach** . . . . page 37
    Evan Ira Farber

**Critique of the Faculty Development and Library
Instruction Movements: A Panel Discussion** . . . . page 67
    Sharon J. Rogers
    John Barber
    George L. Gardiner
    Marilyn D. Ward

**Library Instruction -- The Best Road to Development
for Faculty, Librarians and Students** . . . . page 81
    William K. Stephenson

Contributors . . . . page 85

FOREWORD

As the originator of the subject for the conference from which these papers came, and in the selection of the conference speakers, I have sought to bring together the most authoritative and the most representative opinions in two movements: faculty development and library instruction. My reasons for doing so were the need to establish a dialogue between librarians and professors, and the necessary rapprochement between the two movements. Seemingly, there is no affinity between faculty development and library instruction; the former is faculty-oriented and the latter is student-oriented. However, both movements ultimately benefit the student. The essays of each author address the need for greater understanding between these movements. Each essay offers convincing arguments concerning the value of libraries, including academic multi-media centers, in both endeavors. Patricia Breivik expressed this idea succinctly:

> If library instruction is related to quality research, it is even more directly related to instructional development for better teaching. The goal of instructional development is quality teaching and learning experiences.

Breivik's idea is reaffirmed by all other essayists. This leads me to conclude that the success of both faculty development and library instruction is dependent not only upon greater understanding of the substantive aspects of the two movements, but also upon two other efforst: a spirit of cooperation, and attitudinal change. If this book meets these needs even partially then the efforts will have been worthwhile and the choice of the theme will have had the fulfillment of its goals.

-- Ray R. Suput

Preface

This book of essays grew out of the Twenty--Third Midwest Academic Librarians' Conference, held in May, 1978, at Ball State University. At the close of the conference, the speakers agreed to recast their addresses for publication, and this volume is the result. There have been some title changes, and in a few instances, some substantive changes. One should not consider this book as the proceedings of the conference. The editors, who have the consent of the authors, claim the final responsibility.

– **The editors**

FACULTY DEVELOPMENT IN AN AGE OF UNCERTAINTY

Jesse McCartney

We are here to talk about academic libraries, library instruction, and faculty development and how those topics relate to one another. My charge, as I understand it, is to clarify, if possible, the last of those terms -- faculty development -- and to identify in that academic movement some trends which have implications for librarians and faculty members.

Though academicians are fond of publicly deploring the jargon of bureaucrats and technicians, in truth we spawn new terms and passing fads in academe with such rapidity that we can hardly keep track of our offspring. In fact, some terms and ideas disappear before we ever figure out what they meant or signified. Bradley Sagen, of the University of Iowa, observed in a conversation a few weeks ago that what we need is a kind of educational Dow--Jones Index, so that we could sit down at the end of the day and have a read--out: "Faculty Development -- up two points; Individualized Instruction -- off ½; Evaluation of Teaching -- mixed in heavy trading." I recount Brad's suggestion for two reasons: First, many of us across the country have invested heavily in faculty development and we believe it is a stock which will offer academicians a good return on their investment. But more importantly, Brad's suggestion that we often need a market report reflects a common perception that the academic life these days is a speculative business, full of risks, uncertainties, trade--offs, and fierce competitiveness. Indeed, that perception reflects a new academic ethos out of which faculty development emerged a few short years ago; and in order to understand both that ethos and faculty development, I would like to contrast that perception of academic life against another picture painted in a story by John Updike called, significantly, "A Sense of Shelter."

Updike depicts a protagonist, a high school senior named William, who suddenly discovers that school is a delightfully safe and cozy place. He sees school as a sanctuary, a shelter, a castle in which he reigns as king. He imagines the most romantic interludes a-midst the smell of sweat and galoshes, against the backdrop of fudge-colored concrete blocks and steel stairways, blithely unaware of the plain ugliness of his surroundings. He whizzes through his class work, dawdles around the school building after hours, idolizes even the most loathsome of teachers. He generally sees the whole schooling experience through such rose-colored glasses that he wants it to last forever. In one section of the story, his daydreams reach their glorious apex in the midst of a tawdry study-hall scene. The passage presents a wonderful picture of the dowdyness of adolescence; but it also describes a fantasy which many college teachers have carried with them well into the middle of their careers.

"The two hours of the school afternoon held Latin and a study hall. In study hall, while the five people at the table with him played ticktacktoe and sucked cough drops and yawned, he did all his homework for the next day. He prepared thirty lines of Vergil, Aeneas in the Underworld . . . . He solved ten problems in trigonometry . . . . Lastly, as the snow on a ragged slant drifted down into the cement pits outside the steel-mullioned windows, he read a short story by Edgar Allan Poe. He closed the book softly on the pleasing sonority of its final note of horror, gazed at the red, wet, menthol-scented inner membrane of Judy Whipple's yawn, rimmed with flaking pink lipstick, and yielded his conscience to the snug sense of his work done, of the snow falling, of the warm minutes that walked through their shelter so slowly. The perforated acoustic tiling abo\ his head seemed the lining of a long tube that would go all the way: high school merging into college, college into graduate school, graduate school into teaching at a college – section man, assistant, associate, *full* professor, possessor of a dozen languages and a thousand books, a man brilliant in his forties, wise in his fifties, renowned in his sixties, revered in his seventies, and then retired, sitting in a study lined with acoustical books until time for the last transition from silence to silence, and he would die, like Tennyson, with a copy of "Cymbeline" beside him on the moon-drenched bed."[1]

Well, what can one say? It's a lovely, idyllic fantasy -- one in which, on some Monday mornings, we's very much like to revel. But it just isn't so. The faculty development movement is a response to an ever-growing awareness that, whatever else academic life is, it is not a quiet sanctuary among book-lined studies; it is not a genteel profession where dignity, respect, and accolades (let alone tenure and promotion) automatically accrue to sages who grow wiser with each passing decade. Though we may long for the snug comfort depicted in Williams's study-hall vision, most of the time we recognize that vision for what it is – an adolescent fantasy which is about as far removed from reality as other adolescent fantasies.

However, it has not been easy for us to see that fantasy for what it is. It took Kent State, Jackson State, bombings, protest marches, students' demands for what they called "relevance;" declining enrollments, declining budgets, retrenchment, the firing of tenured faculty members to force some of us to reconsider the realities in which we work and to recognize the need for a renewed examination of teaching and learning. George Bonham, editor--in-chief of *Change Magazine*, recently observed: "Fifteen years ago, [the debate over teaching improvement] was principally left to the pedagogic and ideological radicals -- young student activists in concert with usually hirsute young academics -- their demands for relevance and a new student-learner partnership spilling across their manifestoes. But times changed, and what was once an article of faith of the few self-anointed has now become the concern of a whole generation of academic practitioners."[2]

One of those practitioners who has been a mentor to many of us associated with faculty development is Jerry Gaff, whose book, *Toward Faculty Renewal*, outlines three main streams, strategies, or conceptions of instructional improvement enterprises. It is useful, I believe, to try to clarify what faculty development means in various contexts before proceeding to talk about current trends in that movement. Toward that end of clarifying the term, I have adapted a chart from one in Dr. Gaff's book. This chart, appearing at the end of this paper, distinguishes three alternative conceptions of instructional improvement, any or all of which are sometimes referred to as "faculty development." As the table makes clear, each of these alternatives is characterized by a different focus, purpose, intellectual base, and different acitivites. Since the term "faculty development" has become a more generic term, the conception described in the first column is increasingly referred to as personal or professional development. The other two terms – instructional development and organizational development – have fairly stable meanings.

In a more recent statement in the December, 1977, issues of *Liberal Education*, Jerry Gaff observed: "Faculty development is not new. What is new about professional development for faculty today is the emergence of a conceptual paradigm which provides a different way, a richer way, of thinking about college professors than has been customary. In its simplest formulation, this paradigm holds that faculty members need more than knowledge of their disciplines to be maximally effective in and satisfied with their work".[3]

What, then, beyond the knowledge of their disciplines, do faculty members need? What is it that faculty development tries to provide?

Faculty often need, in the words of Eugene Rice of the University of The Pacific, "a more wholistic conception of what it means to be a college or university professor." In Rice's recent study of Danforth fellows who entered graduate school in the 1950's, a study entitled *Dreams and Realities*, he discovered "extraordinary discontinuity between the patterns of meaning that informed their original dreams, and what it actually meant to teach day--to--day."[4] Despite the fact that most of his subjects were in the middle of what seemed outwardly successful careers in teaching, Rice found them inwardly troubled as a group. Those faculty entered the profession with what was almost a religious sense of vocation. Though that strong sense of altruism may be commended, implicit in that sense of vocation was also the latent desire to be, like the professor in the adolescent's fantasy, "revered." Neither the profession nor its traditions any longer command reverence from society, certainly not from the young. And now such faculty are in search of a strong and meaningful sense of identity within a profession which at least is supportive and purposeful. Many are groping for a more realistic understanding of what it means to be a college teacher in an age of uncertainty. They are searching for a way to live and work productively and fruitfully in tension with change -- change in students, in institutions, and in their own values and shifting career patterns, goals, and aspirations. Rice warns that this search for significance must not become narcissistic; it must help faculty understand each other better as well as themselves, must help them interact more positively with other professionals and understand better the nature of professional relationships.

Such needs are not unique to Danforth fellows. The most popular activity sponsored by the Office of Instructional Development in the nine months that I have served has been a workshop on conflict management. What does that tell us about what it means to be a faculty member today? As I talk with faculty groups here or on other campuses, people say such things as, "I just feel like nobody cares about what I'm doing in the classroom." Or they echo the refrain I've heard so often in the past five years: "They keep changing the rules on me" -- *they* being variously some vague social force, an administrator, or a promotion and tenure committee; *rules* being generally synonymous with the unit mission statement, promotion guidelines, or general expectations of society toward the teacher. I don't think such complaints are whining self-pity. I construe them as genuine expressions of dismay, of a kind of future shock, from people confronted by change and uncertainity; and I think we must take them seriously.

In that same luncheon conversation with Brad Sagen in which he suggested the need for an educational Dow Jones Index, he also ventured to say that he saw faculty development work becoming more and more a kind of secular chaplaincy. He meant, I think, that people working in faculty development would become a kind of combination counselor and Red Cross nurse who could bind up both psychic and physical wounds and send people back into battle. That, incidentally, is legitimate work; I respect it and I think there is some truth in Brad's prediction. However, I would suggest that if we acknowledge a need for that kind of work within the profession of teaching, then we ought to be administering preventive medicine now to graduate students and young faculty members to innoculate them somehow against the kinds of mid--career crises which seem so common among the present faculty. Increasingly, faculty development centers are focusing attention on the apprenticeship phase of becoming a faculty member, the "socialization" process by which one acquires his or her values and attitudes toward the profession.

Through workshops on conflict management, on the clarification and development of values, on inter--personal skills, faculty development encourages personal and professional development. Through the use of growth contracts in which faculty set specific intellectual or professional goals, some faculty development offices encourage personal growth. Through career planning services or retraining programs which allow faculty to switch disciplines or move out of academic life altogether, faculty development programs respect the human needs of faculty and attempt to aid these professionals to find new significance in their work. Bill Berquist and Steve Phillips, co--authors of *A Handbook for Faculty Development*, have plans now for a national re--training center at Berkeley, which will work with faculty, their families and colleagues, and their home institutions as individuals seek to move from one discipline to another in response to institutional needs and personal desires.

But what else do faculty need beyond a knowledge of their disciplines and a sense of purpose and well--being?

Activities sponsored by faculty development programs around the country suggest that faculty need a fuller understanding of and more skill in applying technical tools such as television, computers, and bibliographic and reference tools, especially those which were not available when the faculty member took formal graduate training. Most faculty members need to know more about the psychology of learning and the systematic design of courses of instruction. Workshops in Personalized Systems of Instruction or computer-assisted instruction are common features of faculty development programs. Small group teaching techniques or other alternatives to the traditional lecture method are favorite topics for training sessions. But faculty need librarians who also know about these topics and can communicate effectively with faculty as they seek library resources on these topics or materials which will help them apply these strategies in the classroom. Faculty need learning resources which are more accessible, better coordinated, and more need-oriented. It is not enough that media centers, learning resources centers, and libraries offer service on a take it or leave it basis. They must have programs for discovering faculty and student needs and responding to those often highly individualized needs more affirmatively.

Similarly, faculty need to respond more affirmatively to the individual needs of contemporary students; Joe Katz recently observed that students are a perpetual mystery to faculty. Of course they are; that is why teaching can be so much fun and why it can be so frustrating. Faculty development centers often support activities designed to help faculty learn more about students, but we need not fear that the mystery and the fun will disappear simply because we learn more about student learning styles, personal values, career goals, and attitudes toward teachers and schooling.

Faculty members also need an institutional and organizational context which facilitates meaningful professional activity. Again, quoting Eugene Rice, "It has become clear that the growth and sustained vitality of faculty depends in large measure on institutional support, diversity, and flexibility in program planning. Faculty need to participate in the improvement of established programs and the initiation of new ones. They need to see their ideas actualized institutionally. They need to be able to achieve personal and professional goals through available institutional means, so that both the individuals and the institution benefit."[5] In less loftly and more direct language, I would say that they need effective, imaginative leadership -- department heads, deans, librarians, vice-presidents, computer-center directors, and other institutional managers who respond quickly and positively to their frustions and their aspiration, removing the one and encouraging the other.

Some faculty development programs work with both administrative officers and faculty to create such an environment. This sometimes means providing training for administrators in personnel and fiscal management, in planning and program evaluation, and in facilitation skills; it sometimes means tackling serious institutional problems -- the reward system, the management of human resources, the allocation of space, the development of new curriculum policies, the reworking of the way faculty load is reported, or the evaluation of teaching. But the general purpose of organizatonal development activites is to create a more effective environment for teaching and learning.

Now let me turn for a moment from reading this Dow-Jones report on faculty development acitvities to reading the tea-leaves. Where is faculty development going? How can academic libraries, library instruction programs, and faculty development offices work more constructively to meet present needs and shape the future? How can librarians and faculty become stronger allies in the efforts to improve instruction, futher professional development, and bring about institutional renewal?

Those who have been engaged in faculty development work far longer than I – Joe Katz, David Justice, Jack Noonan, Jack Lindquist, Jerry Gaff -- all suggest that faculty development programs will continue to focus on personal development, instructional development, and organizational development – but at a more subtle and more sophisticated level. They suggest that there will be less emphasis on consciousness-raising and greater emphasis on better-planned, more substantive programs. Jack Noonan, of Virginia Commonwealth University, voiced the sentiment of most of the pioneers in faculty development work when he observed at a recent meeting that the improvement of teaching is far more complex than we have thought it to be. Joe Katz stated in the same forum that teaching is more complex than psychotherapy. Such statements indicate that a less active and more contemplative phase of faculty development is beginning. We'll have fewer short courses and workshops and more on-going explorations of teaching, learning, institutional life, and changes in the profession. We will likely begin to work with graduate students -- the neophytes in the profession – to prepare them better for their teaching roles and for the professional climate in which they will be working. We will encourage greater collaboration in designing courses -- especially in general education which is a hot stock itself at the moment -- collaboration among librarians, faculty development staff, and faculty. Course-related library instruction programs will be one way of promoting this collaboration. Institutions will place more emphasis on effective teaching -- both by measuring it more systematically and rewarding it more equitably. Institutions will gradually begin to deal with the fact, reported in the recent Ladd-Lipset survey, that roughly 40% of faculty are strongly committed to teaching while only 6% report being strongly committed to research.[6] And faculty development programs will be instrumental in bringing about these changes in academic ethos.

The library will remain the symbolic center of academic life, and for those libraries which house media centers, instructional resources, and faculty development programs, as well as printed documents, this central role will be more than symbolic. To assure the centrality of libraries in the academic community, librarians will have to come to a fuller understanding of the new condition of academe I have been describing – a condition in which the only thing constant is change. In order to become stronger allies of other faculty in the effort to improve instruction, to promote professional development, and bring about institutional renewal, librarians will need to become more sensitive to the special stress this new condition puts on persons and on academic systems, and they will need to understand better and respond more humanely to the personal needs generated by this stress. As the focus on teaching grows, the traditional function of libraries as research centers may diminish somewhat. As libraries become actively involved in facilitating instruction (as indeed some of the libraries represented at this gathering already are), they are likely to become noisier and messier and busier in the process. Though I hope they will be able to provide a sense of shelter for the beleagured academic, a cell for the solitary and contemplative life of the mind, a place for reading, reflection, and research, they will also serve as a hospitable haven, a rich resource, for the scholar--teacher and for students who engage in the more active processes of teaching and learning.

ALTERNATE CONCEPTIONS OF INSTRUCTIONAL IMPROVEMENT[7]

	Faculty Development	Instructional Development	Organizational Development
Focus:	Faculty Members	Courses or Curricula	Organization
Purpose:	Promote faculty growth; help faculty members acquire knowledge, skills, sensitivities and techniques related to teaching and learning.	Improve student learning; prepare learning materials; redesign courses; make instruction systematic.	Create effective environment for teaching and learning; improve interpersonal relationships; enhance team functioning; create policies that support effective teaching and learning.
Intellectual Base:	Clinical, developmental, and social psychology; psychiatry; socialization.	Education, instructional media and technology, learning theory, systems theory.	Organizational theory, organizational change; group processes; management theory.
Typical Activities:	Seminars, workshops, conferences on faculty roles as advisor, teacher (manager, collaborator, facilitator, authority figure), person; on evaluation of faculty.	Projects to produce new learning materials or redesign courses; workshops on writing objectives, evaluating students, test-design; small-group learning, techniques, individualized or computer-assisted instruction.	Workshops for group leaders or team members, action research with work groups, task forces to revise organizational policies, clarify mission, evaluate reward system.

FOOTNOTES

1. John Updike, "A Sense of Shelter," in *Modern Short Stories*, ed. by Arthur Mizener, 3rd ed. (New York: W. W. Norton & Company, Inc., 1971), pp. 184-185. Originally appeared in *The New Yorker*, 1960.

2. George W. Bonham, "Foreword," *Evaluating Teaching Improvement Programs*, by William R. O'Connell, Jr. and L. Richard Meeth (New Rochelle, N.Y.: Change Magazine Press, 1978), p. 4.

3. Jerry G. Gaff, "Current Issues in Faculty Development," *Liberal Education*, LXIII, 4 (Dec., 1977), p. 511.

4. R. Eugene Rice, "Response to 'Current Issues in Faculty Development,'" *Liberal Education*, LXIII 4 (Dec., 1977), p. 527.

5. Rice, p. 526.

6. "The Ladd-Lipset Survey," *The Chronicle of Higher Education*, XVI, 5 (Mar. 27, 1978), p. 2.

7. Jerry G. Gaff. *Toward Faculty Renewal* (San Francisco: Jossey-Bass, Inc., 1975), p. 9.

FACULTY DEVELOPMENT FROM A LIBRARIAN'S POINT OF VIEW

Dwight F. Burlingame

The last decade has seen an increasing emphasis on faculty development as a valuable component of academe. Numerous periodical articles, conferences and reports by campus committees deal with faculty development from a wide variety of vantage points. Only recently, however, have academic librarians begun to come to grips with this concern, partly as a result of an increased and broader understanding of their environment. Librarians must, I believe, take advantage of this opportune moment.

In relating my viewpoint on this topic, it is important to note that I do not consider myself an expert in faculty development. Frankly, I believe there are few of those, though some people, including myself, have thought about it a great deal and so have written about it -- most notably Jerry Gaff.

From my perspective, I veiw faculty development as a movement through which librarians will be able to recognize, understand, and survive the forces that at times threaten to overwhelm them. Paraphrasing Emerson, we must listen carefully not to what the Cassandra screams but what the library whispers. Faculty development can also be an instrument to preserve and protect the values in our culture which we wish to transmit. Let us examine how this important movement in higher education today affects librarians and what role they are to play.

The obvious beginning point for the individual is to explore the pertinent literature. A sound theoretical base for faculty development can be found in the behaviorial and management writings of Likert, McGregor, Herzberg, and others. Stone and Marchant have applied the theories to librarianship. Jerry Gaff's classic work, *Toward Faculty Development*, is worth considered and thoughtful reading. The *Chronicle of Higher Education* and *Change* magazine provide information on current topics. With the informed background such reading can provide, librarians will be able to examine and more sharply define their role in the faculty development process. They will be able to encourage development of meaningful and viable programs of service for themselves and other faculty members. They will be able to plan more effectively and productively. They will be able to evaluate programs better in light of today's changes in higher education. Needless to say, strong and wise leadership will be required in our libraries to make positive progress.

What has caused the recent growth of efforts and expenditures under the rubric of faculty development? It certainly has resulted in part from the contraction of the universe of higher education. Librarians are having to ask themselves each day how they can be effective, creative, and challenged at the same time with shrinking resources. Additionally, the changing clientele of our colleges and universities, in particular the adult learner, has caused a re-evaluation of courses, programs, and instructional methods.

Too often the morale problem of the teaching faculty, the plight of the teacher in higher education today, and the financial problems of our faculties are presented as though librarians and administrative faculty do not face similar problems. Librarians and teaching faculty are, after all, part of one institution, each profession contributing its own work and playing its own unique role. Just as teaching faculties find themselves unable at times to work at maximum effectiveness, so do administrators and librarians.

Library faculty, must make the time to take advantage of what faculty development can offer. We in the library world in particular, can no longer afford to sit back and let someone else take care of our needs and wants. It is imperative that we accept, and I emphasize that word, *accept*, our rightful place and at the same time demonstrate our abilities to the faculty development movement.

For librarians, the complexity of faculty development is compounded by its duality. There is a need for clarity in defining not only their role in helping teaching faculty renew themselves, but the role they are to play in their own self-renewal.

Three general areas in which the academic librarian can contribute to the movement are instructional development, research, and library instruction.

Although definitions of instructional development are many and varied, a useful definition is found in the instructional development booklet used at SUNY's Oswego College of Arts & Sciences:

> "The Office of Learning Resources is charged with promoting the increased effectiveness and efficiency of teaching and learning. It is to provide a variety of options to support traditional classroom activities and to encourage the use of alternate learning modes that are most appropriate to help accomplish the goals of all academic programs and other designated

institutional obligations. This office also directs liaison activities between the faculty and the Learning Resources agencies and among agencies themselves."[1]

Librarians have an important role in assisting the faculty in the improvement of instruction. Needless to say our library schools will have to help serve as agents of change. The training for academic librarianship should include courses in research techniques, instructional methods, and learning theory, to name a few. The skills developed by such courses would be most useful as preparation for an active role in faculty development.

Another very natural role which we have played almost from our beginning is that of the librarian in research and thus a role in faculty development. A major area of faculty development is renewal of the faculty member by retooling in his curricular area. The obvious identification of the library as a place for research, and thus a place for a faculty member to renew and develop, needs no further comment.

The third major role is that of library instruction and its related impact. Evan Farber has been most effective over the years in speaking to and demonstrating the effectiveness of course-related library instruction.[2]

In addressing the general topic of the involvement of the library in faculty development, it behooves me to address the issue of library faculty development as well. Through faculty development librarians are not only helping teaching faculty to renew themselves, but are realizing that continuing education is something in which they should also participate. The classic study done by Elizabeth Stone entitled, *Factors Related to the Professional Development of Librarians*, was significant in pointing out that the individual librarian needs to realize that continuing education is something which should be done for oneself.

Librarians must analyze their needs carefully and develop a plan for long term growth which recognizes the importance of auxiliary disciplines in the field of librarianship; that increasingly specialized knowledge needs to be acquired; that the ability to increase one's skills in response to a changing society must be developed; that a concern for ethical values and a sensitivity to human needs enriches everyone; that a need exists to foster a regard for the importance of scholarly endeavors. It is clear that ultimately it is the individual who is responsible for his/her own continuing education. Librarians as well as teaching faculty must be self-corrected. However, they certainly need support from administrators, from librarians, from fellow-colleagues and faculty members, from students, in pursuing their efforts for continued development. The experiments of the Professional Developmental Lead Program at Oakland University in Michigan illustrate one way in which we can proceed. The experience at Indiana University, which has an extensive process which allows for continuing education and staff development, is also illuminating.[3] If we truly profess the belief that the library is central to the educational enterprise, then it logically follows that faculty and academic librarians are partners and not adversaries. They seek a common goal in educating students, and if this is true, then the role that librarians are to play in faculty development is indeed an important one.

At a recent conference on faculty involvement in library instruction, the participants were informed that perhaps only 1/3 of the faculty in higher education have an adequate understanding of the facilities, materials, and services available at their on-campus library. Only a small fraction know what materials are available to them through the library. Therefore it is quite logical to assume that if the teaching faculty knew what was available to them and utilized those materials fully, then the resulting effect on our students would be ever-so-great and we would be putting out a better product.

Therefore, we as librarians, have a most important role in faculty development, if only to acquaint the faculty to optimum utilization of available resources and services. The reluctance of librarians to embark upon faculty orientation programs as well as teaching faculty's reluctance to admit that they might learn something, clearly indicates to me that we need to take action immediately.

The important idea that the reader should learn from this article is that librarians must ready themselves for the challenge that lies ahead. Victor Hugo's often quoted saying, "There is nothing quite so powerful as an idea whose time has come," seems most appropriate. Surely, the idea of faculty development is one whose time has come.

FOOTNOTES

1. J.R. Pfund, *Instructional Development in Perspective* (State University of New York, Oswego College of Arts and Sciences, 1975) ED 121272, p. 6.

2. One of Mr. Farber's notable works in this area is "Library Instruction Throughout the Curriculum: Earlham College Program," in *Educating the Library User*, by John Lubans (New York: R. R. Bowker Co., 1974).

3. Carolyn A. Snyder and Nancy P. Sanders, "Continuing Education and Staff Development: Needs Assessment, Comprehensive Program Planning, and Evaluation," *Journal of Academic Librarianship*, v. 4, no. 3 (July, 1978), pp. 144–150.

THE ROLE OF THE LIBRARIAN IN FACULTY DEVELOPMENT; A PROFESSOR'S POINT OF VIEW

Paul A. Lacey

I was planning to start by saying something about faculty development using Jerry Gaff's definition. Since Dr. McCartney has already quoted Gaff's definition, I can move ahead quickly. Gaff's point is that a faculty development program should have some possibility for influencing each of three areas -- personal and professional development, instructional or curriculum development, and organizational or institutional development. If I think of faculty development in relation to library service, I think of it primarily as related to enhancing the teaching–learning process itself; that is I'm speaking as a classroom teacher about what I want out of faculty development, what I hope I can get in part from my colleagues who are librarians.

I think of a faculty member as both a teacher and a learner, as a user of library resources, and as one who requires others to use library resources. I believe that the goals of a faculty development program ought to be to help people identify what they can do to improve the teaching–learning process. It should help them enjoy what they do more; it should help improve the state of the art of teaching and help raise the level of discourse about teaching and learning. Let me emphasize these goals by saying I want to improve both *performance* and *enjoyment* of teaching and learning. I want to see us find ways to make it possible for colleagues to learn from one another, to share more fully with one another what has been good and satisfying teaching.

Let me consider the rather general goals I have just announced, in relation to the three areas in which faculty development programs should operate: Instructional or curriculum development, organizational or institutional development, and personal or professional development.

Curriculum development involves thinking about such things as course designs, course goals, selection of materials. When I think of curriculum development, I find myself asking, "What do I want students to know, what do I want them to be able to do as a result of taking my course? How can I design the experiences of the course, the sequence of events in the course, so that my students have the best possible opportunity to learn what I want them to learn? What do I assume they start with, what do I assume they can have as foundation for other courses to build on after they have had my course?"

Institutional development may involve considering the same kinds of questions on an institution--wide scale. What do we want out of a liberal arts education? Can our goals best be served through course curricula or through distribution requirements or a totally free elective system? What are the agents of good learning in the institution and the learning milieu created by dormitories, of a dining room, of instructional buildings, of the library? What can we do to support and strengthen the agents of good learning? Are there ways we can organize our curriculum to make more efficient use of resources, to streamline programs, to increase our resources or to allocate them more effectively?

Certainly institutional development can mean anything from examining my course in the context of the whole curriculum, to considering a new calendar, or studying the effect of dormitory life on learning; and here the librarian can be tremendously important in providing materials for thinking about those questions, gathering books and articles together so faculty members and administrators can have easy access to what is going on in the field. In our own case at Earlham, we have a very small faculty lounge in the library and that is a place where such materials are regularly made available. People can browse and read and check things out. We also have brief reviews sometimes of the same kinds of materials in the faculty newsletter. I am sure that is not unique to us. I simply mention it to emphasize that these are ways of making materials available which you already think about all the time, and which might be simply focused a bit more if you are thinking about faculty development.

Personal professional development, which I imagine is what most of your teaching colleagues think about, comes first, for me. I think of this point, when I think of faculty development, both because of my own situation, and because it seems to me to be the starting place for significant work with students. Personal and professional development may mean various things – things as various as getting grants for research in writing, using summer as released time for research, extending one's knowledge of or competence in a field, engaging in seminars or workshops which enhance one's teaching skills. If I had put all those activities under the smallest number of headings, I would say that professional or personal development is concerned with increasing our skills and our satisfactions as teachers and as researchers.

Other things may come from faculty development activities -- promotions, tenure, better jobs, a reputation in one's field, none of which are to be disparaged. But I find it most useful to think in terms of increasing skills and satisfactions, and because I teach in a small undergraduate college I'm going to start there in talking specifically about what I hope to receive from librarians. I will then branch out to speak as best I can to the situation some of you may come from -- the university with its greater emphasis on re--search activities.

For me, the key to both successful teaching and successful learning is being able to frame a significant question. It is what makes a class discussion successful, a research project successful. To frame a question, means making a judgment about what is worth asking on a subject, what will produce the most important connec--tions between ideas and bits of information and what can lead us into more sophisticated or far--reaching questions.

Now, I speak of framing rather than asking questions, for obviously all inquiry begins with simply asking something. What I am trying to get at is the process by which one examines a body of material, or an event, or a phenomenon, and at the same time examines the tools or the means by which a further examination of that event or phenomenon can be best made. Framing the question is not just choosing the best way of expressing a request for infor--mation. It is more like framing up a building, that preliminary roughing out of the space one is going to occupy, putting in the supports which allow one to do the substantial building in a more orderly fashion. I have to consider the materials I have to work with, the terrain I'm working in, the tools I have at my disposal. If I'm framing a question, I have to ask what I want to know, and how I'm likely to find out what I want to know in the most de--pendable and most efficient fashion.

Sometimes the framing is a matter of rephrasing the question, taking advantage of the tools and materials I have, asking questions I can answer as a way of laying a foundation for more complicated or speculative questions. Sometimes framing the question involves inventing new tools to get information not available in any other fashion. Being able to frame the question implies being able to get some satisfactory answer and, as I have said, I believe that to be the key to successful teaching and learning and research. It is what I do when I am doing what I believe to be good scholarship or good criticism. It is what I do when I teach effectively. Here I can put together both curriculum development and professional develop--ment goals.

I ask myself what I want students to be able to do after they have reviewed research, what I want to come out of their writing of papers, and that leads me to thinking how a paper assignment should be constructed. What I am doing, when I am most fully engaged in this kind of reflection, is framing the questions which will organize a course in terms of both what content should be examined and what I want my students to be able to do with the material. This may seem very obvious, but I don't think it is, or if so, that doesn't mean very many of us know what to do about the obvious.

If I am concerned with the art of framing questions, I do not put on my syllabus that each student will write a paper of ten pages on a subject of his or her own choosing and leave the instructions there. Neither do I write examination questions made up of a tendentious quotation and the instruction, "Discuss." You know the sort of thing that I mean. Things like: " 'You can turn a tragedy into a comedy, by having everyone sit down.' Discuss." That's Lord Peter Wimsey. Or, " 'Comedies end with a marriage, tragedies begin with one.' Discuss." That's Lord Byron. The single word *discuss* is not a sufficient frame for a question. That too may be obvious, but it took me a number of years of teaching to learn it, and, if I may say so quietly in this room, I think there are a great many people in education who have not yet learned that. The instruction *discuss* does not provide enough basis even for evaluating the answer, let alone for making the process of answering the question an educative one. If I seem to be laboring an academic point, bear with me, for it leads to talking about how the library and the librarian can help me with the process of framing the question and thereby contribute to my development as a teacher and to faculty development more generally.

We must start, I think, by acknowledging two things: first, that for those of us in the social sciences and the humanities certainly, and for those in the natural sciences pretty substantially, the library is the most important and the largest tool box we have for framing our questions. I am not trying to ignore the existence of laboratories, but I want to argue that the library is the most important and largest tool box we have for framing our questions. That's my first point. The second is: most of us who are teachers and researchers are poorly instructed in how to use the tools the library provides. We think of the library as a warehouse for books rather than a system for information retrieval. We don't know the tools in the library.

What has been our experience as professors, after all? We have been accustomed to having the toughest courses we took and the toughest we teach introduce the longest list of books on reserve. Our professors gave us fine annotated bibliographies and we may do the same for our students. Often it has been our experience that the most challenging graduate seminars we took specified both the paper topics and the works we were to consult for all but the final paper; and frequently the final paper was an outgrowth of one of the shorter papers we did under instruction. That is to say, our best graduate courses in our discipline, like the best undergraduate courses we expected to teach, gave exclusive attention to mastering the content of major works in our field. Except in the rarest cases we were taught to regard the library solely as the place where all those things should be waiting for us.

I think of my very good experiences with reference services in college and graduate school, but I recall that I, and everyone else I knew, tended to go to the reference desk as a last resort and that I asked questions with no notion that I might learn a *generalizable* method of research which could help me become more expert in research and conceive of more interesting questions to pursue, either on my own or with the help of a reference librarian. And, I would add, I do not believe I ever thought of a librarian as a teacher until I began to work at Earlham. Except for the most obvious things, such as using the card catalogue and bibliography if I came across one, each piece of study I did through college and graduate school, if it had a research dimension to it, was essentially another hit or miss, hunt and peck activity. I might become more at home in an area, such as the Romantic Period, which is one of my areas of specialization, so I could cover more material in each subsequent piece of study, but I did not know much if anything about how to branch out efficiently into a new area. My independence as a student and as a thinker was consequently very limited, and I didn't even recognize the fact. I thought of the library as a vast reserve collection where I could find what had been assigned or suggested. If I ran into a puzzle about a date or an event I might go outside the reserve collection, but only rarely would either an assignment or a question I found myself entertaining require that I use unfamiliar materials or devise a strategy for searching out material.

I suggest that my experience is not untypical of both under--graduate and graduate use of the library even now. If I am right in this, it would follow that many of us who are now teaching in colleges and universities are only slightly at home in libraries; and, that being the case, we do not know how to set our students off on interesting and do--able topics which we haven't handled a dozen times before in our course. Nor do we know how to evaluate a library. We are only likely to ask how many books the library has, what percentage of E & G it receives yearly, how many books it adds and how many periodicals it has -- important questions, but not the fundamental ones, I think.

We are like the New Yorker who brags about living in the "Big Apple," but who knows only that part of New York right around his apartment and right around his place of work and along the bus or subway route which connects one with the other. I never had a course in bibliography, though many programs in English will offer one for the first year graduate student, but even at that level the pattern has been to explore only the smallest part of the library's resources, that is, the area around home, the area around work and the route in between them.

I recall a former student telling me with embarrassment that she had gotten an "A" in a graduate bibliography course, taught at a major university by a very well-known scholar and bibliographer. She said she felt the professor rather took a liking to her, when she got the only "A" on the first assignment. The professor had told the class to go to the card cataloque, look up Jane Austen's *Pride and Prejudice* and write down everything that was on the card. My student did just that and was the only student to do so. In fact, since she was a graduate of Earlham, she had learned about tracings and bibliographical notes on the cards, but she wasn't doing anything sophisticated; she was only following orders. And she was the only person in the class to write down exactly everything that was on the card.

Now, I don't make too much of the story; a first assignment has its own problems in any course. But consider: this is a graduate course in bibliography; the assignment is a learning-by-doing one of a fairly low order; it is a very prestigious university in the mid-60's (I don't mean the price range, I mean the year); and exactly one student got the assignment right. Does this tell us anything about the level of library instruction and experience of students and their teachers, I ask rhetorically? I suggest that it does.

When I began teaching I did what I had been taught to do. I put together long reserve lists for advance courses, but rarely designed assignments to require the use of books so identified. I assigned research papers in most general terms and directed students to the texts and critical articles I already knew, rather than encouraging them to conceive of questions or problems which I had not already thought through. And let me emphasize this – I was a good and successful teacher in terms of engaging students with materials and preparing them for graduate school.

It follows from all this, I think, that I did not know how to help my students figure out how to do research, how to distinguish good from bad material to use for research. I used to be terribly frustrated, for example, by the student who wrote a research paper on *Hamlet* which cited Dover Wilson, Ernest Jones, an article from the "Police Gazette" and a privately printed monograph on Bacon as Shakespeare written by a clergyman in Cornwall in 1847, and who treated each source as equally authoritative since they were all in the library. But I didn't know how to explain to that student how to avoid the error the next time, and even now when I read a paper in social sciences which begins as a review of the literature and I see the student going through the material with the thoroughness and lack of discrimination of a powerful vacuum cleaner, I have a sense that my colleagues over there do not know much more about research than any of us did when we first got out of graduate school. My colleagues who assign such papers often lament the amount of garbage being published in their fields. But they apparently see no alternative to wading through every bit of it. They act as though no authority has weight except one's own reading of every piece of research, and they assign papers which are as indiscriminate as they are tedious.

In considering the ways a library can help change that situation, I think of Kenneth Boulding speaking of the technique of indexing information. In his book, *The Meaning of the Twentieth-Century*, he says the discovery of indexing information is one of the great tools for the perception of complex social systems. He says, "It is fundamental to all knowledge processes that we gain knowledge by the orderly loss of information." *We gain knowledge by the orderly loss of information.* Most of us assumed when we first started teaching that you didn't dare lose information. It was always piled on more and more and more; knowledge was always the sum total of all your information. Learning to use a library, learning to use indexing methods, may be among the ways of helping the faculty member keep up with his or her field in a far more efficient fashion than most of us have ever imagined before.

The librarian who can help a faculty member learn to use the tool-box more effectively can make an enormously important contribution to every aspect of faculty development. Probably the librarian who chooses to do this will find it is best done by taking advantage of the library's being viewed as a service function of the institution. That means that you may enter into discussion with individual faculty members or with departments about how to enhance the library's service for specific courses through identifying holdings or designing course-related library instruction. In such a discussion, the librarian can help the faculty member clarify the goals of the course by asking both what the research assignments will be, and what library skills it would be valuable for the student to know. How will the faculty member evaluate the papers? What will the paper have to do in order for the instructor to think it is very well done? How can a student without native skills or a lot of previous experience know how to do his research paper successfully?

In such a conversation, the assignment, the research paper, can become a teaching device, not just a means of evaluation, and the result can be better papers and more satisfaction for the faculty member. Let me emphasize this; I suggest that the beginning of the conversation, when the librarian says, "What may I do for you?" can lead on to a discussion of educational purpose, goals of the course, questions of evaluation, so that the faculty member who, like myself, used to think that "Discuss" was enough of an instruction, recognizes that the teaching process goes on in the instruction about the term paper or the writing assignment, and that it can be clarified, made a better assignment, by saying what the student will want to do or have to do in the library in order to succeed at the assignment.

Such a conversation or series of conversations may also help the faculty member think about his own research interests and the tools he or she doesn't have. Working on library instruction for my students has broadened the kind of questions I now pursue in my own study. I find myself doing what I ask students to do, that is, to ask the most interesting questions you can think of and then imagine the kind of encyclopedia or bibliography which would have to exist to give you some information on that question. That is step one in instructing the student to do a paper for us. It is also step one now for me when I start thinking about a problem. Think of all the possible subject headings under which you might find material on your question and then go to the Library of Congress *Subject Headings* to see which of these headings exist. That is step two for my freshmen and step two for me. I find there is almost always a work corresponding to what I imagined I would need for the research question.

I am quite sure that my greater ability to use the library now is the direct result of years of thinking of the library and of librarians as *primary* resources for improving my teaching.

Let me illustrate my point with two examples from my own work. Last year I was doing some reading in the history of British universities and came across the usual references to the liveliness of dissenting academies in the late eighteenth and nineteenth centuries. I realized that I knew nothing about any of those academies, except for paragraphs here and there about Hackney Academy where William Hazlitt studied and William Godwin and Joseph Priestly had taught.

I decided I wanted to identify a few works which would give me an acquaintance with these academies. But, of course, the history of education in England is well out of my field of competence.

I decided to spend half an hour in the library seeing what I could discover about materials on dissenting academies by following exactly the steps the librarians take when they teach my students to pursue an elementary research strategy! To look in a general and in a specialized encyclopedia; to follow leads and references in such works; to look in the *Subject Headings* of the Library of Congress; to look at tracings on catalogue cards; to look for bibliographies on relevant works – steps one, two, three and four.

I did not intend to be exhaustive in my search. I set the time limit as an experiment in using a search strategy. At the end of that time, I had a list of the fundamental works in the field and enough leads that I could begin a major research project in the subject if I chose to. That is important to me, but even more important is the realization that when I was in graduate school, at the height of my research activities as I saw it then, I could not have accomplished the same thing in days of work. In fact, I probably would have avoided working on the subject simply because I would not have known how to get anything on it. I am a better scholar now because I have read more widely in the years since graduate school but also because I do not have only the hunt and peck approach to a new subject.

The second example is a future work. I've been thinking about a series of lectures I have to give next fall and it occurred to me that one of the topics worth dealing with, since the lectures are on value questions in the humanities, is our understanding of the concept of the conscience.

Often, when we are reading something like Sophocle's *Antigone* in class, my students miss some of the power of the play because they take it for granted that the individual conscience is always to take precedence over the laws of the State. But at the same time, they are unwilling to think of the conscience as the voice of God or as anything but one's deepest held opinions, and I am frustrated at the carelessness of thought when they talk about following the conscience. But I have not been able to achieve much more than to tie my students up in knots by showing them how unsystematic their thinking is.

Now, I have some pretty strong opinions about what the conscience is and how it is best to use the concept in talking to people about problems of conscience. But I realized, as I started thinking about a lecture dealing with that, that I was as unsystematic about the concept as my students are. The only difference is that I have read more, here and there, and have some nice quotations to support my opinions. But, I cannot claim to have studied the usage of the word, or its history as a concept, and therefore I cannot claim to have thought it through as a concept.

All this came to focus for me this week while I was listening to our librarians instructing my freshman humanities class in search strategy and I suddenly realized that there were tools for making a systematic study of a word, an idea, which had to precede my using the word.

The key, here, is systematic study, a new way of framing a question which has not been a question before, but only a set of opinions and prejudices -- very good opinions and prejudices I may say, but heretofore that is all they have been. I now know how to begin such a study and it will be essentially the way my students are studying for their papers.

What can a librarian do for my professional development? I have spoken very self--centeredly here. The librarian can help me feel more at home with the resources of the library, more familiar with all the tools there. The librarian can help me think through what I am doing as a teacher and as a researcher, so I do it better and get more satisfaction out of it. And for me, the place to begin is in helping me frame the question, learn search strategies and minimize the waste and tedium of the preliminary stages of re-- search, that is, surveys of literature as though no one has gone over the ground before -- or fumbling around after information. And then moving from the teaching -- now to my own research -- helping me with all of this learn how to keep up with the discipline more efficiently.

I am not one of those people who is very good at keeping up. People of my generation who came out of graduate school all went around saying the great problem is keeping up, keeping up. We all pretended we were physicists. That was, after all, the post--sputnik era, so everybody had to pretend to be doing something scientific. And so you had people in literature say "if an article gets by it's gone forever. You've fallen behind -- you'll never keep up." Well, friends that's mostly a lie about the humanities; you catch–up, you fall behind. The professor who reads everything or insists that reading everything is the key, probably is not the most effective teacher, at least for an undergraduate audience. And quite possibly that professor isn't the most effective scholar in the field because, if Boulding is right, you have to figure out how to make your loss of information orderly as you go for more knowledge. That seems to me to be a very important fact that librarians can help me with; to learn to use the library, to learn to keep up, is a matter of losing information in the process of gaining knowledge.

There is another stage in the teaching--learning process which Alfred North Whitehead speaks to: he calls it turning knowledge into wisdom. Whether anyone can help us to that stage, I do not know, but I do not put it outside the realm of possibility that it may be a by-product of faculty development. Whitehead also says that wisdom is the way you hold knowledge, and in that respect, anyway, it may be that librarians can be as much help to us who are teaching as anybody.

If I think about the library, now, as a learning milieu, it seems to me it says a great deal about ways we may develop. One comes into a library with an idea of what one wants which may be very vague, very general. A librarian tends to facilitate the processes of clarification by giving help and advice about what one can find on the original question or helping one reshape the question. In the process of describing the interests or assignments and learning what the library can best provide, the student may have his or her wants refined and redirected. The librarian is in a marvelous position almost always to be facilitator but not evaluator. This is a very supportive role which many of us in the classroom covet. We would rather be facilitators than evaluators. That role puts the librarian in a marvelous position with regard to both students and faculty colleagues. The librarian using the resources of the library, as I have already suggested, can have an enormous impact on raising the level of discourse, putting the books and materials around for people to find.

And then, to speak very briefly on the institutional level, it seems to me that the librarian and library resources can be tremendously helpful in at least two areas. One is to help generate new resources. When I was in administration, one of the things I pressed very hard was to ask, when faculty would come with a new proposal for a course or for a sequence of courses, "how is that going to impact on the library resources? Get some money for that too." That is important for a couple of reasons. First, it meant that people on campus thought, "oh yes, we need books for what we are about to do, they don't just happen." It also meant that people thought through at an earlier stage how they were planning this program so it did have an impact on the library. In our experience it also was very helpful in getting the resources, that is in getting the proposal funded. Some agencies were so surprised that a college would think about how the library affected the teaching that they gave us the money just for the novelty of the thing.

It seems to me to be very important how the librarian can be the servant of the institution in the best possible sense and that is through serving the teaching-learning process. The librarians can be important in generating educational ideas as departments think through how they spend their budgets, what to have and why to have it; the librarian can help academics move from impulse buying of books and periodicals, insistence on specialized periodicals for a single person's interests, by helping that faculty member or department reflect on the purposes of the holdings in an entirely new way.

If it is to be a place that enhances faculty development, the library must be, above all, an inviting place where people want to gather, a place where important issues are discussed and materials are left around for raising the level of the discourse, a service center where librarians make the job of research as rational and as convenient as possible, and a place where teaching and learning are modelled by the way people do their work.

LIBRARY INSTRUCTION AND INSTRUCTIONAL DEVELOPMENT

Patricia Senn Breivik

Many concerns are facing classroom faculty and librarians today. There is the question of what declining enrollments will mean and what the ultimate effects of the later retirement age will have on the job market. Concerns for promotion, tenure, and re-tooling are becoming matters of bread and butter, life and death.

There is the constantly changing educational base from which we operate: one day we are concerned with training the best in our country for professional careers; the next day, we are concerned with open admissions and everyone's right to higher education. No sooner do we begin adjusting our activities to conform to the latter philosophy than Harvard comes along with its decision that higher education must have higher standards for undergraduate education. Historians tell us that the swings of the pendulum come ever more quickly, and it is only reasonable to expect that our campuses will no sooner adjust to Harvard's direction than they will be directed back to the concerns of the educationally disadvantaged. Or, if we go to Poe instead of the historians, each swing of the pendulum comes closer to hitting home with faculty responsibilities as educators and with their professional commitments.

Besides declining enrollments, later retirements, and the changing game rules, we are also confronted with the nontraditional student, and I do not mean just the educationally disadvantaged. On most campuses more and more women can be seen returning to school on their way back to the labor force. More and more people are retiring at earlier ages and coming to us for retooling to enter new careers; frequently they have years more work experience than the professors. These people have little patience with poor teaching or with learning experiences that bear little relation to their lives. These students are creating pressures on faculty both within and without the library.

But somehow, within this changing environment, there comes a better opportunity than ever before to expand library instructional programs and for us, as librarians, to become involved in the educational mainstream of our institutions. I saw it happen in New York City when overnight the starting date for open admissions was moved up by five years. No one was ready, the old ways just could not work, and somehow within the extenuating circumstances faculty were more open to trying new ways. More frequently we observe this phenomenon in individual faculty as they come up for tenure. All of a sudden they are concerned about student evaluation of their teaching and about publishing.

Just how does library instruction relate to the two areas which concern most faculty, namely, research and teaching? At Sangamon State University we emphasize that there should be a very close relationship between research and teaching and, perhaps with the exception of the very large research universities, there are growing pressures in this direction. How can someone continue to do good teaching and be completely out of touch with what is going on in his or her field? On the other hand, just to be able to do research will not make up for being a poor teacher. Library instruction, I believe, can play a vital role in strengthening the bond between research and quality teaching.

How can libraries support research besides providing organized resources? Libraries that have active instructional programs can give people a broader awareness of the resources available, they can help faculty get better access to them and provide the faculty with some evaluation skills for the materials. When appropriate, librarians can, and should, direct students to commercially available data bases, resources on other campuses and in the broader community, and help facilitate student use of these resources.

As a digression, let me comment that these are roles that libraries have always had, and perhaps they do not sound like library instruction activities. Most librarians do not think of library instruction as occurring at the reference desk either, but basically librarians have always been involved in teaching and library instruction just in the normal course of being good reference librarians. The difference is that, given the faculty and student ratio to librarians, library instruction has to take place on more than a one-to-one basis. There must be new instructional approaches that will insure that greater numbers of faculty and students can develop efficient library skills to support research and instruction activities.

Library service and library instruction are so intricately involved that it is hard to see the beginning or end of one or the other. For instance, the more library instruction a library offers, the more demands will be made for library services. I shall give you just one example in the research area. Sangamon State is located in the state capitol and has a public affairs mandate. Frequently, when a new research project was undertaken, our librarians, researchers, and students would come up against the same problem: one would know of something that was happening in one place, someone else would know about something else in another or about a piece of information stored in a particular agency. While they could pool what they knew collectively about available resources, they were always wondering how many more resources were in existence without their knowledge. The need became apparent for some sort of clearinghouse on government-related information. The SSU Library has recently received approval from the Illinois Board of Higher Education to establish an Intergovernmental Clearinghouse that would allow for a new public service activity as well as for more efficient and more complete research on our campus; we want to create a government-related information referral system to assist our faculty and students in doing their jobs better. Once it is established, our faculty and students will experience another dimension of quality library services that will back up their projects, not only at the university, but with their government jobs.

I would like to quote the head of one of our research centers at Sangamon State University, who spoke about a major research grant his center had received.

> "We had two librarians participating in a research project from the very beginning. The bottom line of that incident was that it constituted a major savings in the time required to do the literature review. We figured that we saved upwards of three weeks for five or six persons involved in that project, simply by asking the two librarians to take us on a short-cut to the materials. They did it in a way that we could never have done it on our own, and so they have used that as a model for other projects that the center undertakes."

Now this is an example of library instruction. Not only were the faculty members, researchers, and students made aware, in an efficient way, of the literature with which they were to be concerned, but there was also some learning going on in the affective domain, namely, that the librarian was a valuable member of that team, and that the librarian could help them save time and provide more complete access to the materials that would help them do what they wanted to do -- their research project -- better and more quickly.

If library instruction is related to quality research, it is even more directly related to instructional development for better teaching. The goal of instructional development actually is quality teaching and learning experience. What are the qualities of good teaching? I think most people know them instinctively even if they have not had a course on that topic.

A good learning experience will approximate reality. That is why lectures are terribly ineffective. Lectures, reading lists and reserves are far removed from real life. Once students graduate, no one is going to lecture them everytime they need to learn something new on their jobs. No one will hand them a reading list. No one will put books on reserve for them in the public library. Traditional teaching methods are far removed from the realities which will confront people when they leave our campuses.

On the other hand, library instruction, that is teaching people an awareness of the literature in their fields, how to access it, evaluate it, and utilize it, prepares students for the post--graduation, real--life situations they will encounter. It will prepare them to cope with the multi--media sources of information that are so much a part of society today. It will prepare them for the mass media that bombards them everywhere they go. Faculty and librarians working together can help students learn how to deal with the existing plethora of information. Together they can create what our instructional development friends would say is a positive learning experience, because it is close to reality.

Another quality of a good learning experience is that it is active, not passive. Again, the lecture method is the antithesis of this quality, even allowing for question and answer periods. Educators have said for years that students should be provided with op--portunities to learn by discovery -- discovering concepts from specific incidents and in varying contexts. Then there is problem solving – getting students to start with an initial problem and to think it through so that the process becomes an active, not a passive, learning situation. Library or research skills obviously have a part to play in this process. Once students have acquired basic information handling skills, they can begin to frame their questions about the problem; they find the information that relates to those questions and decide what is important or what needs to be done. This, again, is closer to what students will face in life when they get out of school; and it is also an active process, not a passive one.

We also know that *good learning or teaching is individualized*. Young people reach our college campuses with a thirteen year spread in academic ability -- a thirteen year spread in reading and math abilities. How can any one reading list be effective for any group of thirty students? We are forced to look again for other ways of learning -- ways to individualize the process. Again, by taking students directly to the resources of the academic library and community, new doors open whereby professors can individu--alize the learning/teaching process for their students. The richness of resources allows students to deal with topics that are closer to their areas of interest. It allows students to vary the materials they use to accomodate their reading levels. A student with a reading deficiency can concentrate on a couple of magazine articles instead of reading two thick books on a topic, and thus have time to go over the material repeatedly until it is mastered. If the only way a student can learn something is by hearing a professor say it one time, the great majority of our students are lost.

Building on preferred learning styles is possible for students if there is access to the many resources of multi-media-based libraries or resource centers. Some students learn best by listening, some by seeing, some in a lab situation; some work better in groups and some individually. Once faculty free themselves from the lecture, the textbook, and the reading list, and start looking for alternate approaches that utilize multi-media resources, multiple approaches to learning can become a reality on our campuses.

Part of *good teaching is up-to-date-ness*, and we know how quickly information is being out-dated. In fact, educators have been saying clearly, for some time, that the only valid object of education today is to concentrate on learning processes -- not on content. The cliché is *life-long learning*. Almost every college catalogue states as one of its institutional goals, the preparation of people for life-long learning. This is where library instruction becomes essential. If young people can acquire an awareness of the literature of their fields, how it comes packaged, how to access pertinent information from that literature, how to evaluate it, how to organize and use it, is not that really preparing people for life-long learning? Is it not insuring that their education does not have to stop once they get their diploma?

All of these points that I have touched upon -- having the learning experience close to reality, having it be an active process, making it individualized, concentrating on process rather than content -- build toward higher motivation for the student in the learning process. Psychologists tell us that *students learn best when the threat level in the environment is very low*. Once professors begin using approaches that allow students to learn by discovery, to take a problem and work it out, they remove from the student the pressure of trying to figure out what the professor really wants. Under traditional approaches, students know that the professor wants something quite specific to be accomplished, but they spend a lot of time trying to second-guess the professor, just as reference librarians do when students come in with questions for an assignment which neither the librarian nor the student can understand. Taking this threat away from students (it will take teamwork between classroom faculty and the librarian) and allowing them to learn by exploring materials themselves will provide a more positive learning experience. Educators tell us this is one of the best ways to increase students' motivation to learn.

Incidentally, this approach also takes a lot of pressure off the faculty member. It is a terrible thing to have to be the fount of all knowledge on a subject. How much nicer for faculty to become comfortable as facilitators of learning, to help direct students, to get them started, and then to expose them to the literature to find out on their own (something librarians have known about for quite a while). This takes from the professors the burden of having to know everything or of having to keep the students' attentions so narrowly focused that the students will not go beyond the professor's realm of knowledge. It also helps with motivation because students can see the relationship between the process they are using (particularly if it is pointed out to them) and what will be facing them once they get out of college. Most studies show that 50% -- 80% of what is learned in courses is forgotten by students within a year. These frightening figures add importance to the fact that preparing people for life--long learning is what higher education has to be about today. The acquisition of information handling skills is not a luxury; it is a necessity.

Library instruction can help promote better teaching in all these ways, but it will happen only if librarians can help relate library instruction to the faculty's instructional objectives for their students. Most faculty's knowledge of the learning process and instructional objective setting is somewhat limited. Most faculty, after all, have their training in a subejct area; most of them have not been trained in instructional development or curriculum design.

Since, therefore, librarians cannot assume that most faculty really set learning objectives for their courses, asking faculty what their learning objectives for a particular course are may well run the risk of embarrassing them. Nontheless, we librarians have always dealt with these kinds of situations. In reference interviews users often state needs inexactly and then we question and probe until we help them arrive at a precise statement of what they want to know or accomplish. We already have the basic interpersonal skills to help faculty who do not know how to set learning objectives to articulate them so that we can begin helping them in a more effective way. This assumes, of course, that we know something about setting learning objectives or that we are willing to learn.

Such an approach presupposes that we do not come to the faculty with a pre--determined library instruction package. However, I am afraid that many librarians are guilty of doing just that. Most library instructional programs are one--faceted. One campus will use self-paced workbooks, one will have workshops built into courses, one will have point-of-use tools. Why has this occurred? In most cases, very conscientious librarians working at reference desks have discerned real educational needs and have dealt with them in the manner with which they were most comfortable. They have forced all instructional requests into one delivery format. The approach to faculty then is not, "Let's work out together what best meets your instructional objectives," but, "Here is what we will do for you, take it or leave it."

The possibilities are quite varied. Let me run through some of them very quickly and then pick examples from our university just to show that on an individual campus, librarians can come up with a multifaceted approach to library instruction. (I must confess that there are some instructional approaches that we have not even touched upon in the library program at Sangamon State. For instance, we have no point-of-use library instruction as yet, and this is an area that we need to explore seriously at some point.)

Our communications program came under stern admonition a couple of years ago for lack of "intellectual content." As the communications faculty were sitting around one day concerning themselves about getting some "intellectual content" into the curriculum, the librarian who is on that curriculum planning committee said, "Why don't you let me try?" This opening led to the development of a workshop in the basic communications course that would expose the students to the wide range of resource tools related to their studies. (Of course, it helped that the librarian was there when the discussion was held. At Sangamon State a librarian is assigned as liaison to every academic program and thus sits on every curriculum planning program on the campus.) The communications program tried the workshop and was not totally convinced it was worthwhile, but while the faculty were thinking about dropping it, the students indicated on their end-of-semester course evaluations that the library workshop was the thing they liked best and thought was most worthwhile. It now has a permanent place in that basic course. Many of the academic programs at SSU have similar overview-of-the-literature and basic-access-tools type of workshops built into one or more courses.

We also have workshops of a different kind for particular course areas in which a need exists for some specialized knowledge and information handling skills. In the general management program and in the community arts management program, there is a need to be able to raise money. To help meet that need, one of our librarians gives a workshop on fund-raising sources and how to access them. Another librarian gives workshops on how to present information effectively by using audio-visual aids; however, he gives a very different workshop in the teacher preparation sequence from the one he does in the management program.

In some instances librarians team teach courses with other members of the faculty. Such courses have included "Legal Research and Writing," "Demography," and "Relevance of Professional Literature." Occasionally there is a demand for full courses to be taught by librarians. Two such recent courses were titled "Government Publications and Their Use" and "Grants: Stalking the Great Green Dollars." The librarians have offered tutorials regularly; however, these have proven to be so time consuming that they are now undertaken only under special circumstances.

Other instructional efforts include the production of guides to resources, required workshops for all graduate assistants within the university, workshops for secretaries, and some serious in-house efforts to upgrade the knowledge and skills of both the professional and support staffs of the library. University-wide workshops were held to prepare the campus for the new copyright law, and the media study center offers instruction, on an individual and group basis, to learn how to operate basic AV equipment (a requirement for all communications students) and how to do basic AV production.

Currently we are in the process of setting up three instructional stations on the main floor of the library in the reference/catalog area. As occurs at most libraries, many workshops are held in the library proper. Because it is impossible for more than a few students at a time to see an index citation or the wording on a catalog card, a bank of transparencies is being prepared that provides enlargements of a wide range of examples to illustrate lectures. The multiple location of overhead projectors and screens that pull down from the ceiling will allow maximum location flexibility.

There are, indeed, many approaches to library instruction that can be used by librarians in support of faculty's research and instructional development activities. This support can be significant, but before it can become a reality, most librarians will have to be personally involved in instructional development to enhance their own abilities. The outcome of such efforts will eventually result, I strongly believe, in better learning and teaching experiences on our campuses.

BIBLIOGRAPHIC INSTRUCTION AT EARLHAM: A COOPERATIVE COURSE--RELATED APPROACH

Evan Ira Farber

One can go through the stacks and through files of periodicals such as *Improving College and University Teaching* or the *Journal of Higher Education* and find literally thousands of pieces of advice on teaching undergraduates. Perhaps one thing many of them agree on is that the beginning point is Mark Hopkins and one student, but even then they don't agree. If you look in different quotation books, one of them reads, "Give me a log hut with only a simple bench, Mark Hopkins on one end, and I on the other and you may have all the buildings, apparatus, and libraries without him." It *is* agreed that James A. Garfield, who was a Williams alumnus, gave this address in talking to Williams College alumni in 1871. I always heard it as "a log with Mark Hopkins on one end and me on the other is all the college I need." Whatever the version is, let us agree that one ideal is Mark Hopkins and one student. Others, though, believe Socrates is the starting point. But whomever one begins with, Mark Hopkins or Socrates, from then on there is almost no consensus in the literature on what are the most effective methods of teaching. There is, however, a great deal of repetition and repli-- cation of experience. Some of these may prove helpful, but too many of them are depressingly similar to those nondescript, unused collections of sermons that so many of us have in another area of the stacks.

If one can draw any generalization from this mass of materials, from the range of methods and devices, it is simply the obvious one, that no single method is best, and that the method or methods adopted must take into consideration the possible variations in the three components of the teaching--learning process: first, the instructor, with his or her individual personality, ability, training and educational philosophy; second, the content of the course, its subject matter, materials, and objectives; and third, the students, their number, level of experience, abilities and interests.

What I want to show here is how at one institution, Earlham, some commonly used teaching methods – the lecture, written exercises, individualized instruction, discussion groups, problem solving assignments, and sometimes several of these in combination -- have been used in bibliographic instruction, not only making that instruction more effective, but at the same time, helping the teaching--learning process itself become more effective. However, keep in mind that what we have done is not completely appropriate for your institutions; at the same time, you can use our experience, which has been successful, I think, and adapt it to your own situation.

Our approach to bibliographic instruction is course--related; that is, we do not believe in a separate course, a course in bibliography, or in use of the library, or whatever term may be used. Our approach, the course--related approach, was really motivated initially by the realities of academic life. That is, courses in particular disciplines or over several disciplines are the standard ingredients of the curriculum. They are what faculty and students are interested in. They are what academia is mostly concerned with.

About five years ago I wrote that bibliographic instruction through departmental or interdepartmental courses may be a temporary expedient until a clearer and better grounded theory for it can be worked out, or until the teaching faculty wholeheartedly accepts library instruction as a valid part of the curriculum. I've changed my mind. Our experience since then has convinced me (at least for now) that giving bibliographic instruction through existing courses is for a number of reasons even preferable to giving bibliographic instruction as a separate course. But – and this an important *caveat* -- it must be effective, interesting and given not at just one level or in one discipline, but structured so that it becomes increasingly sophisticated as students advance and develop in their capabilities, and it must extend throughout the curriculum. Our faculty, for the most part, has accepted this. Why then are there still problems? These are problems that are faced even after the most difficult hurdle is past; that hurdle, that most difficult one for every instruction librarian is, of course, simply gaining entry into the classroom, but that's another story.

Let's assume for our purposes here, that that hurdle has been passed and we're now in the classroom. What then are the problems that I am talking about? There are those resulting from a brief appearance, distracting the main thrust of the course, presenting complicated, yet prosaic material in a short time that does not have immediate reinforcement. Let me expand on these a bit.

First, bibliographic instruction is usually a one--shot effort. There is no opportunity for developing a relationship. The classroom instructor gets to know the students, their likes, their dislikes, their idiosyncrasies, and vice--versa; they get to know his or hers, and adjustments can be made to create a better teaching–learning environment. An instructor in a classroom can begin badly or even have occasional bad days, but he can make it up over a period of time. The instructional librarian, on the other hand, has usually just one period to have a positive impact. Second, the material is not inherently interesting. Generalizing about information retrieval is difficult and it is not made any easier when students don't know how little they know. Third, the goals of bibliographic instruction, the teaching of search strategy, the development of the ability to discriminate among kinds and sources of information, to become intelligent information consumers, are peripheral to students. Teaching them how to find information usually stands between them and their assignments -- at least they perceive this initially. Fourth, many assignments are just not well constructed or explained, or they are unreasonable in terms of their library demands, but the instruction librarian has to do his or her best with them. Finally, search strategy can be subverted really, if students want to short--circuit it and the class instructor is not really observant.

These problems must be recognized; all of them can be overcome, but it takes careful planning and effective presentation to do it. One result of this planning is a variety of library--related assignments that are alternatives to the term paper. Some of these are shown in Appendix I of this report. Almost all of these assignments were developed through consultation between librarians and faculty about the objectives of the course, about the scheduling of assignments, about projects and librarians' presentations. We'll come back to these, but before that let me show how different teaching methods have been applied to bibliographic instruction.

First, the lecture. I suspect that most bibliographic instruction is given by this form and, as a matter of fact, it used to be almost the only way we presented material. Other techniques are often used now because they've been proven more useful. Why do we still use the lecture technique, especially if it's true that college students can learn as much from printed materials as they can from a lecture? More in some cases, since each individual can go at his or her own pace, can reread, if necessary. The rationale is that readings must be aimed at the average or typical student whereas a lecturer can plan for a particular class, a particular group of students, and can respond to that group as the lecture proceeds. Lecturing, according to Wilbert McKeachie of the University of Michigan, (perhaps the most widely regarded expert on college teaching), is most likely to be effective in situations where there is considerable variation between groups in ability, relevant background or motivation, and where flexible adjustment to groups is important. Course--related instruction through lectures, incidentally, is also advantageous because it personalizes the librarian, identifies the librarian with the teaching--learning process. It points out the instructional librarian as someone whom students can later seek out and seek out confidently because they have already established some kind of relationship.

McKeachie also notes that the lecture should start with a problem, one which is meaningful to the student, presented in such a way that the student feels a need for problem solving. This is difficult to do in giving bibliographic instruction because each student has his or her own topic to research or his own problem to investigate. We've tried to accomplish it by taking a typical problem and showing how one should pursue it. The example shown in Appendix II is pages of the handouts that accompany a bibliographic lecture to a course in Educational Psychology. The first five pages consist of the reference works and suggested subject headings, something about the card catalogue, all of which should be useful to a student who's doing, in this case, a research paper. We provide large sheets that show portions of different reference works, giving in this way an example of search strategy for a topic that a student in this course might well choose.

What we try to do -- and this is done in may of our lectures -- is to take a typical problem and show how one should pursue it, to show in other words, the search strategy for the particular subject. The bibliography distributed gives the students a descriptive listing of the reference works they may use. The sample search provides the problem with the steps toward the solution. It presents the material from the viewpoint of the student.

Appendix III is the educational psychology library assignment. It may not be immediately apparent to students how to apply the principles described in the lecture to their particular topics, since what we've presented them with is a method or theory of search. As Pat Breivik said earlier, the most effective way of learning is by doing and so for many courses we now use exercises that, in most cases, take the form of a work sheet that provides step-by-step guidance for a student's individual topic. After completing these, the students bring them into the library for a reference librarian to look over. In this way feedback is provided, feedback that includes correction, explanation and reinforcement. Appendix IV, is just another worksheet for another course, Foundations of Education. We use a similar worksheet for most courses, but adjust them to the assignment, to the needs of that particular course. So this is another kind of instruction, individualized instruction, but used in conjunction with, or as a follow--up to, the lecture presentation.

The ideal of individualized instruction, as I quoted before, is

Mark Hopkins and a student, but a more common example is the Oxford tutor and the single student who, usually over glasses of sherry, discuss the books the student has been given to read the week before and the paper he had written during the week. It's a great system for those lucky enough to attend Oxford or Cambridge. Who, after all, would not revel in the company of C. P. Snow or C.S. Lewis or one of the other great Oxford dons? As enviable as this might seem, I am not so sure it was always so good. Also it is a very expensive form of instruction and can only be considered at all feasible when the intellectual sophistication of the student is very high. It would hardly be appropriate to apply this situation to a beginning student of literature who had not yet learned to write an essay, or who did not have the basic familiarity with the major literary figures. It would be, in other words, a deplorable waste of time and talent of someone like C. P. Snow or C. S. Lewis.

The parallel with bibliographic instruction is the use of an experienced reference librarian to teach individual students the basic facts of using the card catalogue or the elements of search strategy or how to use the *Reader's Guide*. One--to--one reference service can be an effective educational experience. But it's a luxury that few libraries can afford much of, and even if one can afford much of it, it doesn't make sense to apply it to beginners, just as it doesn't make sense for C. S. Lewis to work with students who know nothing of English literature. It really should be applied only after the student has learned the basics, has begun working on his or her own. The basics should be taught to the group and then the reference librarian can work with individuals.

This is what we've tried to do, by first giving students worksheets to fill out on their individual topics, which they can then discuss with their reference librarians. Several years ago, when Billy Wilkinson, who is now at the University of Illinois, Chicago Circle, did his dissertation in a comparative study of undergraduate reference service at four institutions -- Cornell, Michigan, Swarthmore and Earlham -- one of the things he found was that Earlham students ask much more sophisticated questions of the reference librarians. The reason for that, of course, was that the simple, elementary kinds of information that reference librarians at other institutions gave to individuals, Earlham librarians gave to groups. Our students, then, are prepared to ask more sophisticated questions. We give individual help, in other words, but structure the bibliographic instruction so that the help is most effective and thus more efficient.

Now, let me go over a few of these other examples of alternatives to the term paper.

Let's take the third one as a good example of problem solving. This was a course in children's literature. This assignment was developed by myself and the person who taught Children's Literature. We were trying to find a way by which we could introduce students to library materials that would teach them something about the reference materials for children's literature and at the same time provide them with a meaningful, pleasurable experience. We came up with this assignment: Each student was given one hundred dollars to spend to build a classroom library. They were to describe the kind of school it was, the grade level, etc., and then justify the titles they chose for that hundred dollars. To do this, they had to become familiar with *Children's Books in Print*, with sources of reviews of children's books, and many of the other reference works about children's literature. It was an interesting assignment and perhaps even a practical one.

Notice that the assignments described on these pages are not confined to any one discipline, but range over all of them – psychology, education, political science, cross-disciplinary courses, Japanese culture, animal behavior, American foreign policy, ancient Greek philosophy, introduction to philosophy. Nor are they confined to the beginning classes or to senior classes, but extend to all levels.

As you can see in Appendix V, the project in Political Science 24, Introduction to American Politics, is designed to develop an understanding of the process of American government through direct research in the primary documents. Now, this course and the library work integrated into it represents for me the ideal of course-related bibliographic instruction, where the objective, to develop in students an understanding of the process of government in the United States, and the objective of bibliographic instruction – teaching students the materials and methods for information retrieval, become mutually reinforcing. If I had more space I would have liked to expand on that statement because I think that ideal is worth understanding and discussing in detail.

You can see the idea of the course was to have students follow the legislative process from a bill's conception through its culmination usually in the adjudication of an act by the Supreme Court. In each stage of that process students would have to find the primary documents – the Congressional, executive, and judicial documents. The worksheet illustrated in Appendix VI shows all the information that one particular student (a freshman, incidentally) got on that particular piece of legislation, the Voting Rights Act Amendments of 1970. Three lectures on the organization and bibliography of documents were given to this class, along with an extensive bibliography and samples of documents and reference tools. And as we have discovered with other courses where students are required to find and work with primary sources, the interest level, even the excitement, of students was very high.

From the library's viewpoint and the teacher's viewpoint, this was a most successful course. Those students, most of whom were freshmen, with some sophomores, will be better prepared for work in any of the social sciences because of their familiarity with government documents.

The two flow charts in Appendices VII and VIII are other kinds of instruction that we use. There is one of simplified search strategy for undergraduate biology students and the other is how to find literary criticism in book reviews. I am sure many of you will have questions about the validity of some of the responses on that flow chart, but that's not the point, rather their purpose is to show students that there is a systematic, a logical way of looking for information, one that can be diagrammed.

All the preceding remarks show just a few kinds of assignments that can help teach use of the library. They require different styles, different content, different objectives, and each was devised taking into consideration the characteristics of the particular course to which they were related.

The nature of post-industrial societies is much speculated on, but certainly one of its most salient characteristics is going to be that it's an information-based one. That information, however, is useful only insofar as it is transformed into knowledge, that is, information that has been systematized and organized. The major task of academic librarians and of teachers working with librarians is to convey that knowledge, to show how and why it has been organized, so that so that students who will be living in that society can become intelligent, critical consumers of information, to cope effectively with continuing change in their lives and their professions and their roles as citizens. That ability to cope with the future is certainly a major objective of education, of the teaching-learning process. What I hope I've shown here is how bibliographic instruction can enhance that process, how institutional librarians, by interacting with the teaching faculty, can help shape more effective, more interesting assignments.

One of the things we've discovered is that most faculty appreciate this help. As one of them said, librarians are a non-threatening group to teaching faculty, and, in discussing assignments in preparation for bibliographic instruction, can serve as a sounding board. For the first time, perhaps, a faculty member will have an opportunity to talk about shaping a particular course – what its objectives, its assignment, and its structure are. By suggesting assignments that will help achieve those objectives, librarians may also help the faculty member articulate the shape of the course. By working with faculty in helping shape assignments, courses can be made more interesting and more effective. And by doing this, bibliographic instruction will contribute to creating for the library and for librarians a much more integral part and a much more important role in the teaching–learning process which, after all, is what higher education is all about.

APPENDIX I.

ALTERNATIVES TO THE TERM PAPER: A VARIETY OF LIBRARY--BASED ASSIGNMENTS (EARLHAM COLLEGE)

1. Psychological Processes. (The methods course, required of all psych majors. Mostly sophomores.) The professor chose a number of very specific psychological phenomena that had been treated in review articles several years ago (e.g., Rapid eye movement during sleep); each student was given one of these and had to update the review, using such tools as *Annual Review of Psychology, Psychological Abstracts* and *Social Sciences Citation Index.*

2. American Government. Students use an assignment sheet to guide them in using government documents to trace a law through the legislative process. They also report a test case of that law in the U.S. Supreme Court.

3. Children's Literature. Each student pretends to have $100 with which to buy children's books for an imaginary class which they describe. They then use various selection tools to spend that sum most effectively.

4. Japan in the Twentieth Century. Students read two books on the same topic and write critical reviews which included quotations from other book reviews.

5. Japanese Culture. For this course students were asked to do all the work for a term paper except for writing the first, second, and final drafts. At various times they turned in: 1) their choice of topic; 2) an annotated bibliography; 3) an outline; 4) a thesis statement; 5) a first paragraph and a conclusion.

6. Animal Behavior. Students were asked to design an experiment in the field of animal behavior nutrition that would attempt to ask and answer a meaningful question, one that might be funded by a government agency or a research institute. Students were to find an appropriate funding agency, figure out the costs involved, and then submit a proposal describing their project, along with a supportive annotated bibliography. Groups of students acted as reviewers for the proposals. (A similar assignment, without having students do the laboratory research, was

given in a lower division course in Human Nutrition.)

7. American Foreign Policy. In the professor's words:
Your assignment for this term is to work in groups of three and to assemble and critically evaluate material from public and government information sources on a particular foreign policy issue. At three different times during the term you will turn in a different part of this project, with the entire opus due on May 23. Accompanying your annotated bibliography at that time will be about a 15-page interpretive essay on the material and your topic which examines the ideological conflicts over the issue; a brief history of the issue; the actors involved in the policy formulation process; the other foreign policy issues to which your topic is linked; and a brief statement about the future of your foreign policy issue.

8. Ancient Greek Philosophy. In the professor's words:
Select a pre--Socratic philosopher you find interesting (pick arbitarily if none interests you, or drop the course). Go to the library and read the fragments in translation (on reserve). *Then find two differing interpretations of his work.* Read them and write a paper discussing how they use the evidence to justify their interpretations. Be sure to state which you find more convincing and why.

9. Introduction to Philosophy. In the professor's words:
Your principal assignment for this week is a library assignment closely connected with paper no. 2: Jim Kennedy will provide library instruction. You will then go to the library and find several *important* articles on "affirmative action." Be sure that the articles do not all take the same position. Then, (1) Prepare an annotated bibliography of those articles (due 11/4), and (2) write a paper analyzing the two most important *differing* articles, relating them to your own ethical theory as you began to develop it in the paper on sexual ethics. Make any modifications in your theory called for by the need to deal with the problem of discrimination, or by the arguments studied in the two weeks on Kant. The paper is due at the beginning of class on November 7.

10. Biology 58: Plant Kingdom. In the professor's words:
Within the first few days of this course you will be assigned (quite randomly) the responsibility for dealing with

a plant division (*i.e.*, the Bryophta). You are asked to do the following:

(A). Find out what are the major reference resources *viz,* journals, monographs, reference volumes, etc., dealing with your division of plants.

(B). Find out "Who's doing what to which and where" *i.e.* document who and where are the major contributors within a given group; what is the *direction* (*i.e.* physiological, systematic, morphological, etc.) of their research programs.

(C). Find out (with your newly acquired perspective gained in parts (A) and (B)) and list *three* major questions applicable to your group that you feel have not been resolved, yet need to be spoken to. Please justify your selection of these unanswered questions. Parts A, B, and C are to be prepared in handout form to be shared with your classmates. (The Xeroxing is on the department!)

(D). Finally, prepare a 15 minute *oral* presentation – no reading please!! – to be given before your classmates (and other interested students?) on a research report dealing with your plant group that you feel is *representative* of the type of research that is currently being accomplished. This oral presentation, accompanied by the appropriate visual aids, and followed by a 5 minute question period will be given in seminar form during the latter portion of the term. Details TBA.

APPENDIX II.

EDUCATIONAL PSYCHOLOGY

Basic Reference Sources in Lilly Library, Earlham College

February, 1974

ENCYCLOPEDIAS, HANDBOOKS, AND YEARBOOKS

Encyclopedia of Education. 10 vols. 1971. Ref/LB/15/E4
    Another of the excellent Macmillan Company encyclo--pedias, this contains articles by almost 1,000 contributors, among whom are the leading authorities in their respective fields. The articles are fairly lengthy, providing excellent intro--ductions to, and overviews of the particular subjects; almost all contain choice bibliographies, ranging from just a few items to extensive listings. Be sure to use the index volume first: in addition to the index, it contains a "Guide to Articles" which provides many "see also" references. Perhaps the best place to begin for research on a topic whose terrain is unfamiliar.

Encyclopedia of Educational Research. 4th ed., 1969. Ref/LB/E4.8/1969
    A massive work -- over 1,500 pages -- it is "designed to pro--vide a convenient source of information about most of the important aspects of education," from the most theoretical to the very practical, and covering all levels. Each articles is written by an authority and attempts to review the important research in the field, citing each article or book that the author considered important. It provides, then, a survey of thinking and research plus an extensive bibliography for each of the topics covered. Though arranged alphabetically, one should use the index which is on the yellow pages in the middle of the book.

Annual Review of Psychology. v.1, 1950-- On counter--height index shelves.
    Each volume contains 13 to 18 reviews of the literature in various topical areas of psychology. Since 1958 the plan has been to present certain important topics (e.g., Developmental Psychology, Psychotherapy) each year; others will appear every second, third, or fourth year and a few irregularly -- all depend--ing on their importance and amount of new literature. The bibliographical essay on each subject covered is by an authority

in the field. They cover the important literature and emphasize interpretation and evaluation. There are author and subject indexes in each volume as well as 5-year cumulative indexes of chapter titles. The library has volume 1 to date. Exceptionally useful for keeping up with recent developments in particular areas of psychology. Chapters on "instructional psychology" appear in volumes 15, 18, 20, and 23.

Buros, Oscar Krisen, ed. *The Seventh Mental Measurements Yearbook.* 1972. Ref/Z/5814/PB/B9.32

This source consists of two main parts: "Tests and Reviews" and "Books and Reviews." This latest edition lists 1,157 tests that are commercially available, 798 critical test reviews by 439 reviewers, 181 excerpts from reviews of tests which first appeared in 39 journals, and bibliographies of references. The tests cover psychological, vocational, and educational subjects. The reviewers, who are mostly college teachers of education and psychology, sometimes differ in their evaluations of the tests. A 140-page section of indexes includes an index of test titles, an index of names, and a classified index of tests. The work often refers back to earlier editions for further information on a test. This is an extremely important source for anyone using published tests because many tests which make high claims for themselves are judged to have questionable validity.

Psychological Abstracts. 1927-- On counter-height index shelves.

Published by the American Psychological Association, it is the leading abstracting medium in the field. Issued monthly through 1953, then bi-monthly, it is again a monthly beginning with 1966. The 1972 volumes contain some 24,000 abstracts from literature in psychology and allied subjects of interest to psychologists. Coverage includes books, reviews and discussion papers as well as articles and reports in over 700 domestic and foreign journals. Though many languages are covered, abstracts are all in English. Abstracts of research literature give briefly the problem, method, subjects used and principal results and conclusions. Abstracts give the principal topics and points of view presented. The abstracts are signed, but noncritical; the time lag between the appearance of an article and its abstract is about a year. There is an author and a brief subject index in each issue, and an annual author and more detailed subject index for each bound volume. The library has volume (1940) to date.

A problem with using *Psychological Abstracts* has been the lack of depth in its indexing. Over 200 items have been listed in the semiannual indexes under certain broad terms, such as "depression." This problem is largely solved beginning with the January 1973 issue, which uses 4,000 indexing terms instead of the 800 previously used. In addition, the January, 1973, issue expands from 11 to 17 the categories under which abstracts are arranged. A guide to using the improved *Psychological Abstracts* is also included in the January, 1973 issue.

INDEXES AND ABSTRACTS

Education Index. A cumulative author and subject index to a selected list of educational periodicals, books, and pamphlets. 1929 to date. Counter--height shelves.

"The purpose of the *Education Index* is to serve as a clear--ing house for educational literature, with emphasis on that published in periodicals." -- Preface. Besides indexing complete--ly the purely educational periodicals, the editors include refer--ences to educational articles in periodicals which are indexed in the *Readers' Guide* and other Wilson indexes. It lists many of the publications of the United States Office of Education, and since this Office is one of the most prolific and important publishers in the field, the inclusion of its publications in this index is a great help. Entries are under author and subject, with complete information under author. Before July 1961 and after June 1969, reviews of books are under the heading "Book Reviews." Published monthly except June and August, the issues cumulate at intervals until annual volumes are formed. From July 1961 to June 1969 author entries were not included.

Current Index to Journals in Education. Vol. 1, 1969 to date. Shelved on counter--height shelves.

This monthly is a companion to ERIC's *Research in Education* and uses the same subject headings, which differ from those in *Education Index*, described above. Similar in purpose to *Education Index*, but it currently covers over 500 periodicals, about twice as many as *Education Index*. The main entry is given under broad subject categories and cites author and title of periodical articles, along with periodical titles, volumes, dates, and pages. Subject and author indexes cite EJ numbers which refer to articles listed under the main entry. EJ numbers run in numerical order down the pages of the main entry section, e.g., EJ006978, EJ006979, EJ006980, etc. Annual cumulations.

Educational Resources Information Center (ERIC). *Research in*

Education. Shelved on counter-height shelves. The library has v.1, 1966 to date.

A monthly abstract journal reporting on newly funded research projects supported by the U.S. Office of Education. It also includes other research reports and documents of educational significance, regardless of source. Each citation gives the price of a microfiche or a hard copy of the document. The nearest library receiving the microfiche is Miami University, about 25 miles away. Indexed by subject, author or investigator, and institution. An annual cumulative index is published separately.

Educational Resources Information Center (ERIC). *Thesaurus of ERIC Descriptors.* 4th ed., 1972. (On counter-height shelves)

This is a guide to the subject headings used in *Research in Education* and in *Current Index to Journals in Education,* both of which are described above. "Descriptor" is simply computerese for "subject heading." It is similar in purpose and format to the subject heading book shelved between the two halves of the card catalog. "UF" is the abbreviation for "Used For," which is the same as a "See" reference. "NT" stands for "Narrower Term," "BT" for "Broader Term," and "RT" for "Related Term." "NT," "BT," and "RT" are all "See also" references. Important for making the best use of ERIC.

Perceptual Cognitive Development. v. 3-6, 1967--70. On counter-height index shelves.

A bi-monthly which ceased publication in 1970, this bibliographic information service was devoted to "the scientific study and dissemination of information about perceptual, cognitive, and creative processes." Produced on a computer from punched paper tape input, each issue contains five parts: 1) a listing of all types of publications and parts of publications, including even book reviews and dissertations, plus oral reports, arranged alphabetically by author; 2) a keyword--in--context index to all the titles in the previous listing; 3) a listing of all authors, with the addresses of senior authors; 4) a listing of the journals covered; 5) book notices, a section that describes, in fairly extensive annotations, the more important books in the area published during the period. In 1967 some 4600 items were listed, and in 1968, almost 10,000.

Child Development Abstracts and Bibliography. v. 1, 1927-- Ref/HQ/750/A1/C4.7

Issued three times a year by the Society for Research in Child Development, Inc. Consists of two major parts. The first, and by far the larger, is rather full abstracts of articles from about 140 American and foreign journals covering all aspects -- medical, physiological, psychological, sociological, educational, etc. – of child development. A second part, Book Notices, gives lengthy summaries of important books in the field published during the period covered. There is an author index for each issue and a subject index for the year. The library has only volume 34 (1960) to date.

BIBLIOGRAPHIES

Wright, Logan. *Bibliography on Human Intelligence: An Extensive Bibliography.* 1969. Ref/Z/7204/15/W7.4

This comprehensive lists cites 6,736 books, articles, dissertations, etc., on the topic of human intelligence. Arranged by author, with a topical index. No annotations.

Booth, Robert, E., and others. *Culturally Disadvantaged, a Bibliography and Keyword--Out--Of--Context Index.* 1967. Ref/Z/5814/C5.2/C8

This book is both a bibliography of and index to the literature relating to the culturally (or economically) disadvantaged. It was compiled by searching periodical indexes, monographs, books, research reports, microfiche, and related informational sources for pertinent materials. The first part of this book consists of the subject index arranged alphabetically by keywords and the second part of this work contains full bibliographical citations for material appearing in the subject index.

CARD CATALOG

For guidance in using the subject catalog, be sure to consult *Subject Headings Used in the Dictionary Catalogs of the Library of Congress.* Almost all subject headings used in Lilly Library may be found in this book, which is on the counter between the two sections of the card catalog.

Below is a list of subject headings which seem most relevant to this course.

	Approximate Number of Books
Ability grouping in education	5
Educational psychology	50
See also Mental tests	25
Ego (Psychology)	1
Intellect	20
Learning, Psychology of	50
See also Conditioned response	10
Personality	120
Programmed instruction	15
Self	15
Socially handicapped children–Education	20

SELECTED PERIODICALS

The library receives over 100 journals in the fields of Psychology and Education. These are a few most pertinent to this course.

  Child Development
  Childhood Education
  Educational and Psychological Measurement
  Journal of Educational Psychology
  Journal of Educational Research
  Review of Educational Research

APPENDIX III.

EDUCATIONAL PSYCHOLOGY

Library Assignment, Earlham College

April 1977

Name _____

What topic have you chosen for your term paper?

To begin your working bibliography, go to the library and supply the following information relative to the topic above. Use "Educational Psychology; Basic Reference Sources in Lilly Library" but do *not* ask for help from the reference staff.

Answer the following questions to the best of your ability.

1. Which encyclopedias, handbooks, and yearbooks (pages 1 and 2 of "Educational Psychology; Basic Reference Sources in Lilly Library") have introductions to your topic? (List title, volume number and page.) Also cite the volume and page on which any useful bibliography appears.

2. What are the appropriate subject headings (page 5) under which books on your topic are listed in the subject portion of the card catalog? (List the headings in order of relevance, and indicate whether the heading is "highly relevant," "relevant," "related," or "general area.")

3. Which bibliographies (p.2) list information on your topic? (List the title and page.)

4. Locate one relevant periodical article in *Education Index* (p. 2). Under what subject heading did you find it? _____

   _____
   Use the *Thesaurus of ERIC Descriptors* (p. 3) and *Current Index to Journals in Education* (p. 3) to locate another relevant periodical article. What descriptor did you use? _____ What is the EJ number of the article? _____

5. Use the *Thesaurus of ERIC Descriptors* (p. 3) and *Resources in Education* (p. 3) to locate the abstract of one ERIC document on your topic. What descriptor did you use? What is the ED number of the document?

6. Use the *Thesaurus of Psychological Index Terms* (p. 3) and *Psychological Abstracts* (p. 4) to locate one abstract on your topic. In which volume of *Psychological Abstracts* did you find the abstract _____ and what is the abstract number? _____

7. Under what key words do you find a useful article in which volume of the Permuterm Index of *Social Sciences Citation Index* (p. 5)?

       Key words:

       Volume:

       Cite the article found (using the Source Index):

8. Use the Citation Index to locate a relevant article in *Social Sciences Citation Index*. What citation led to what source in which volume of *SSCI?*

Citation:

Source:

Volume (year) of *SSCI*:

This assignment is due at the Reference Desk by_____ .

Your paper will be returned in a few days. If you need speical help, a note will ask you to stop by the Reference Desk.

APPENDIX IV.

EDUCATION 11: FOUNDATIONS OF EDUCATION

Library Assignment, Earlham College

April 1975

Name _____

What topic have you chosen for your term paper?

To begin your working bibliography, go to the library and supply the following information relative to the topic above. Use "Basic Reference Sources in Education Available in Lilly Library" but do *not* ask for help from the reference staff.

Shortly after you have attempted to answer these questions you will have a brief session with a Reference Librarian who will go over each of your answers in an attempt to remedy your individual weaknesses in the use of the library.

Answer the following questions to the best of your ability.

1. Which encyclopedias (pages 1 and 2 of Basic Reference Sources in Education) have introductions to your topic? (List title, volume number and page.) Also cite the volume and page on which any useful bibliography appears.

2. What are the appropriate subject headings (page 5) under which books on your topic are listed in the subject portion of the card catalog? (list the headings in order of relevance, and indicate whether the heading is "highly relevant", "relevant", "related", or "general area".)

3. Which bibliographies (pp. 2, 3) list information sources on your topic? (List the title and page.)

4. Which periodical indexes (pp. 3–5) list useful materials on your topic? Under what subject heading do these materials appear? (List below the titles of those indexes you *checked*. After each title list the subject heading(s) under which the useful material was found.)

5. Use the *Thesaurus of ERIC Descriptors* (p. 4) and *Research in Education* (p. 4) to locate the abstract of one ERIC document on your topic? What descriptor did you use? What is the ED number of the document?

6. Use the *United States Government Publications: Monthly Catalog* (p. 7) to locate a citation for one government document on your topic or in the general area of your topic. What is its Superintendent of Documents number?

This assignment is due at the Reference Desk by _____.

APPENDIX V.

POLITICAL SCIENCE 24: INTRODUCTION TO AMERICAN POLITICS

Term Project, Earlham College

Term II, 1977

I. *Purposes*

1. This project is designed to develop an understanding of the *process* of government in the United States through direct research in the primary documents of that government. You will examine in detail the development of an idea or a proposal from its inception in Congress or the Executive, through its legislative career in both Houses of Congress, to its final adjudication by the Supreme Court. This study will be accompanied, of course, by the normal classroom lectures and discussion and by the reading of secondary texts.

    The final term paper will be a narrative which analyzes the particular aspects of the process which had significance in the outcome of your bill. It is hoped that this study will provide you with a more intimate and "first-hand" knowledge and "feel" for the governmental process than would be gleaned by the secondary sources only.

2. The principal resources for this term project will be government documents. Our library is an official Government Depository, which means that we receive as a matter of course a significant amount of the material published by the U.S. Government Printing Office. The Government produces an awesome amount of material which is of great use to students of American politics and society, but which is often not fully used or understood by many who are unaware of the extent and scope of information available or who are turned away by their inability to use government documents.

    Knowledge of the skills of information retrieval in these valuable sources can be a major research tool to students of political science. A second purpose of this term project, therefore, is to develop these skills in the discovery and use of government documents and relevant reference material in the library.

II. *Procedures*

1. In the first week of class you will be assigned your piece of legislation, a bill which meets certain basic criteria for the study (the legislation must have been adjudicated by the Supreme Court and must have been of sufficient importance and controversy as to have produced committee hearings and floor debate.)

2. Three class sessions (listed in your syllabus) will be devoted to library bibliographical instruction in search techniques and the use of government documents. This instruction, provided jointly by me and a member of the library staff, will cover basic reference materials, as well as the nature and use of congressional, executive, and judicial documents. Additional informal workshops will be provided as needed to answer questions and offer assistance in developing your skills in finding your way through the government documents section.

NOTE: The instruction in specific documents (congressional, executive, and judicial) is scheduled to accompany *classroom* attention to each branch of government. You are strongly urged to begin work on your project early so as to gain the advantage of this "cross-fertilization" and to avoid the competition for documents which might occur if everyone were to wait until the last minute. The project cannot be accomplished effectively if it is done hastily under the pressure of an imminent deadline!

3. The best place to begin the project is by consulting two reference works: *Congressional Quarterly Almanac* and *Congressional Information Service (CIS) Index*. These publications contain their own "legislative histories" of your bill, plus containing much valuable information with which to begin your research. Study these works to become familiar with the nature and subject of your bill. It will help you later on.

4. The final narrative account which you are to produce (the deadline is listed in the syllabus) should be approximately 10–12 pages in length, typed and double-spaced. The narrative should concentrate upon an analysis of the *process* of government rather than upon the *substance* of your specific bill, although some of the latter will be necessary

in order to accomplish the former. (You might include a summary of the bill's substance as an appendix, but it is not desirable to do a detailed analysis of what may well be a long and complex bill.)

You should present a chronological and/or topical analysis of the significant steps in the process, noting, for example, the importance of the clash of interests at committee hearings, the effects of particular procedures (filibuster, Rules Committee action, parliamentary maneuvers, etc.), the influence of key individuals or groups (the President, bureaucrats, floor leaders, committees, committee chairmen, subject experts, etc.).

One of your tasks will be that of *synthesis* of a sizeable amount of raw data (committee and subcommittee hearings, floor debates, executive documents, a Court opinion). CQ and CIS will be of some help in indicating the major points of significance; you can use them as guides to important testimony or crucial procedures along the way. Yet they are no substitute for the use of the primary documents themselves; and it is a test of composition to produce a short (10–12 page) account from a wealth of available information.

5. I and the library staff will be available to provide assistance. Call on us, we are pleased to help. Additional information will be provided in regular class and in the library instruction sessions.

APPENDIX VI.

POLITICAL SCIENCE 24: INTRODUCTION TO AMERICAN POLITICS
Federal Publications Project, Earlham College

Name: *Sally Freshman*

On this worksheet trace the history of your designated public law from its inception in the political process to its adjudication by the Supreme Court of the United States. *Type or write legibly* the information requested below. Examine and note the unique features of each publication used to familiarize yourself with all elements of your search.

Any of the sources listed on the *Federal Publications* bibliography may be helpful and there is no need to consult other works. Make note of the checklist at the end of the bibliography for help with your search strategy. Should you need further help, feel free to ask a reference librarian or consult one of the document guides listed in the bibliography.

Title of Act: *Voting Rights Act Amendments of 1970*

Bill Number

   House: *HR 4249*
   Senate: *used House bill number*

Date Introduced

   House: *Jan. 23, 1969*
   Senate: *Dec. 15, 1969*
   Conference: ---

Date Reported

   House: *July 28, 1969*
   Senate: *Mar. 1, 1970*
   Conference: ---

Introduced by (full name, state, political party)

   House: *Hon. Emanuel Celler (D.N.Y.)*
   Senate: *Legislative Clerk*

Committee Referred to

   House: *Committee on the Judiciary -- Sub. No. 5*
   Senate: *Judiciary Committee Sub-committee on Constitutional Rights*

Number of Co-sponsors

   House:
   Senate: ---
   Senate: ---

Date of Passage

   House: *Dec. 11, 1969*
   June 17, 1970
   Senate: *March 13, 1970*

Page of Congressional Record of passage

   House: *38535--38537 (Vol. 115)*
   20199--20200 (Vol. 116)
   Senate: *7336 (Vol. 116)*

Related bills incorporated into existing act or otherwise dropped

   House: *H.R. 5181, H.R. 5538, H.R. 7510, H.R. 11856, H.R. 12695*
   Senate: *S. 818, S. 2456, S. 2029, S. 2507*

Final Vote Totals
   House: *234--179, 272--132*
   Senate: *64--12*

Date Approved as Public Law: *June 22, 1970*
Public Law Number: *PL 91--285*
Date and Action by President: *Richard M. Nixon, June 22, 1970*

Citation to locate public law in STATUTES AT LARGE: *84 Stat. 314*

Citation to locate public law in UNITED STATES CODE: *42§§ 1973*

Citation to U.S. REPORTS: *400 US 112* What is its case name? *Oregon vs. Mitchel*

When was the case argued? *Oct. 19, 1970* When was the case decided? *Dec. 21, 1970*

Who wrote the majority opinion? *Justice Hugo Black*

Who wrote dissenting opinions? *Chief Justice Warren Burger*

If this was an amendment, to what public law is it amended? *PL 89--110*

What is its common name? *The Voting Rights Act of 1965*

APPENDIX VII.

SIMPLIFIED SEARCH STRATEGY FOR UNDERGRADUATE BIOLOGY STUDENTS

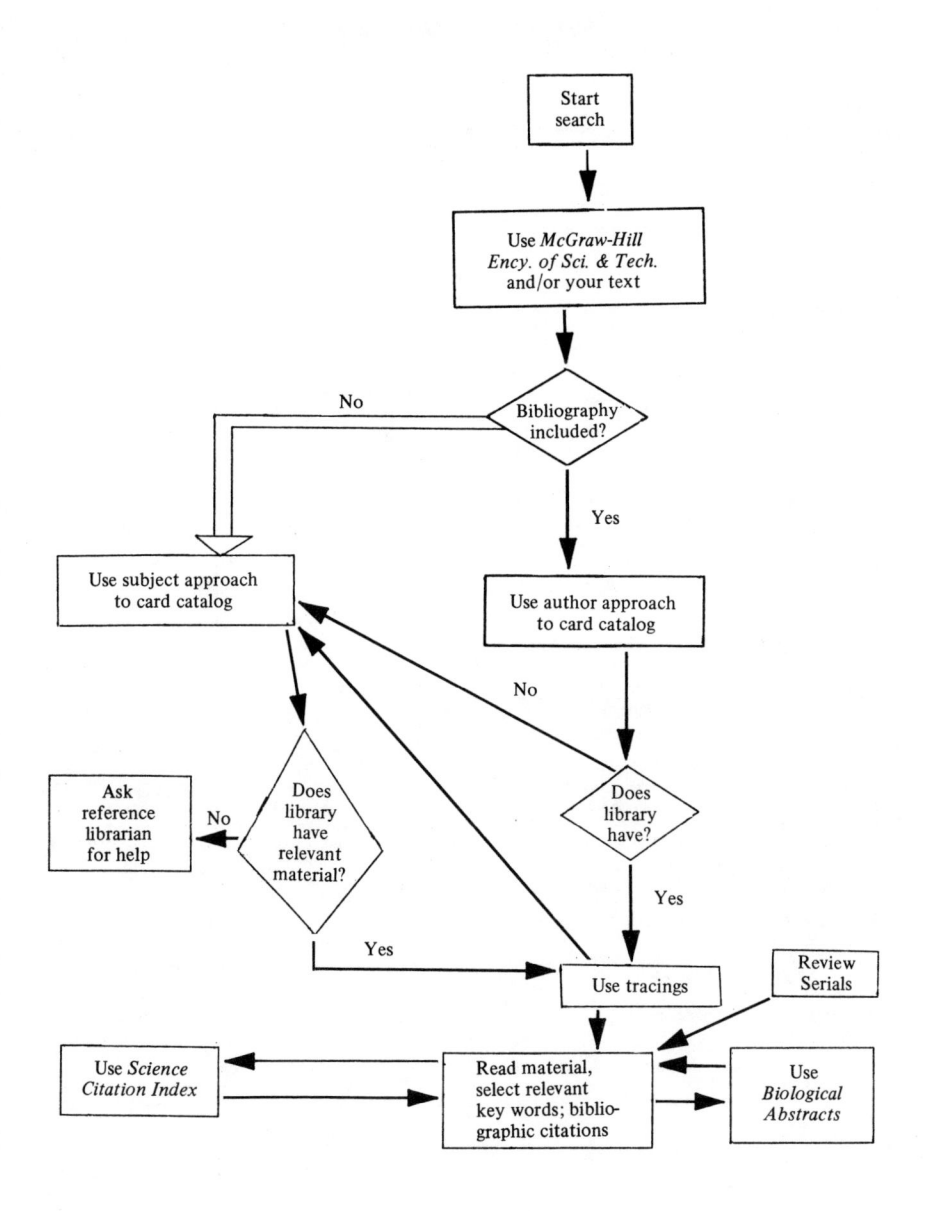

APPENDIX VIII.

HOW TO FIND LITERARY CRITICISM AND BOOK REVIEWS

Earlham College Library

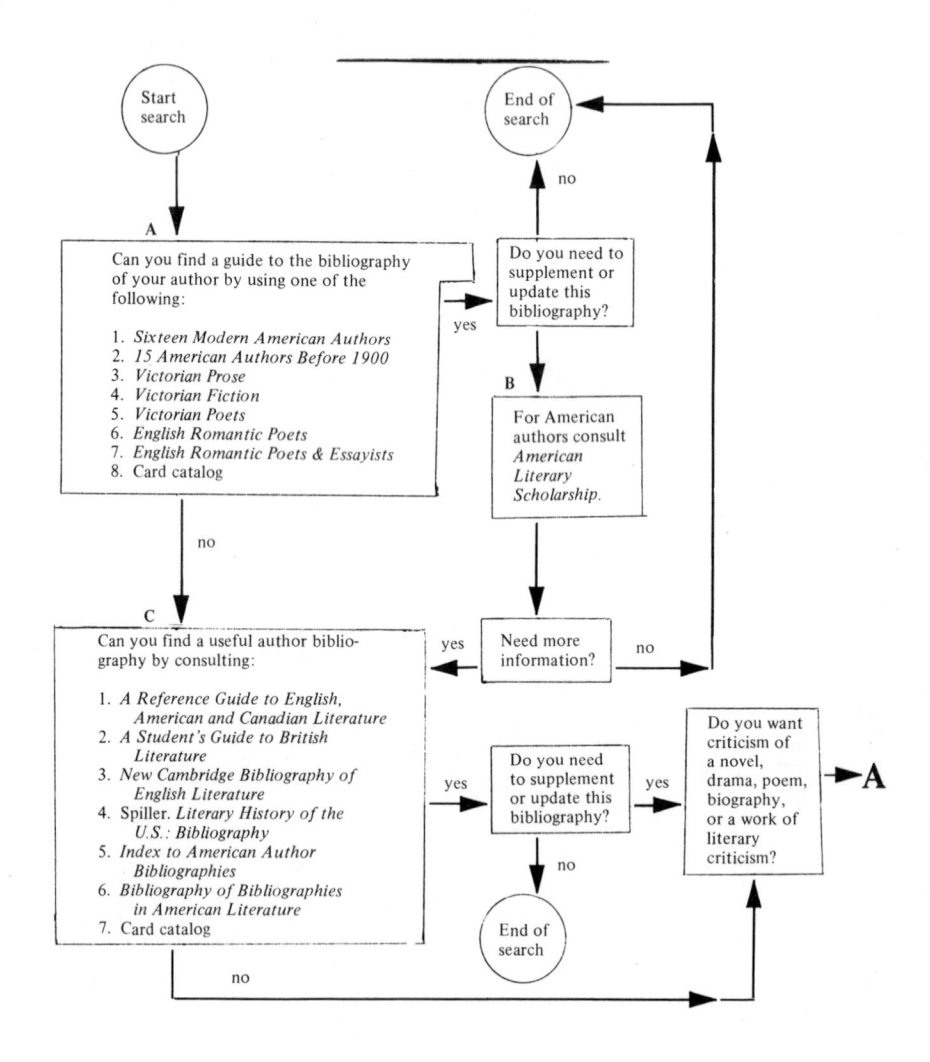

Start search → **A**

A. Can you find a guide to the bibliography of your author by using one of the following:

1. *Sixteen Modern American Authors*
2. *15 American Authors Before 1900*
3. *Victorian Prose*
4. *Victorian Fiction*
5. *Victorian Poets*
6. *English Romantic Poets*
7. *English Romantic Poets & Essayists*
8. Card catalog

— yes → Do you need to supplement or update this bibliography?

B. For American authors consult *American Literary Scholarship*.

Need more information? — yes → Do you need to supplement or update this bibliography? — yes → Do you want criticism of a novel, drama, poem, biography, or a work of literary criticism? → **A**

— no → End of search

C. (no from A) Can you find a useful author bibliography by consulting:

1. *A Reference Guide to English, American and Canadian Literature*
2. *A Student's Guide to British Literature*
3. *New Cambridge Bibliography of English Literature*
4. Spiller. *Literary History of the U.S.: Bibliography*
5. *Index to American Author Bibliographies*
6. *Bibliography of Bibliographies in American Literature*
7. Card catalog

— yes → Do you need to supplement or update this bibliography?

— no → (to Do you want criticism...)

End of search

APPENDIX VIII continued –

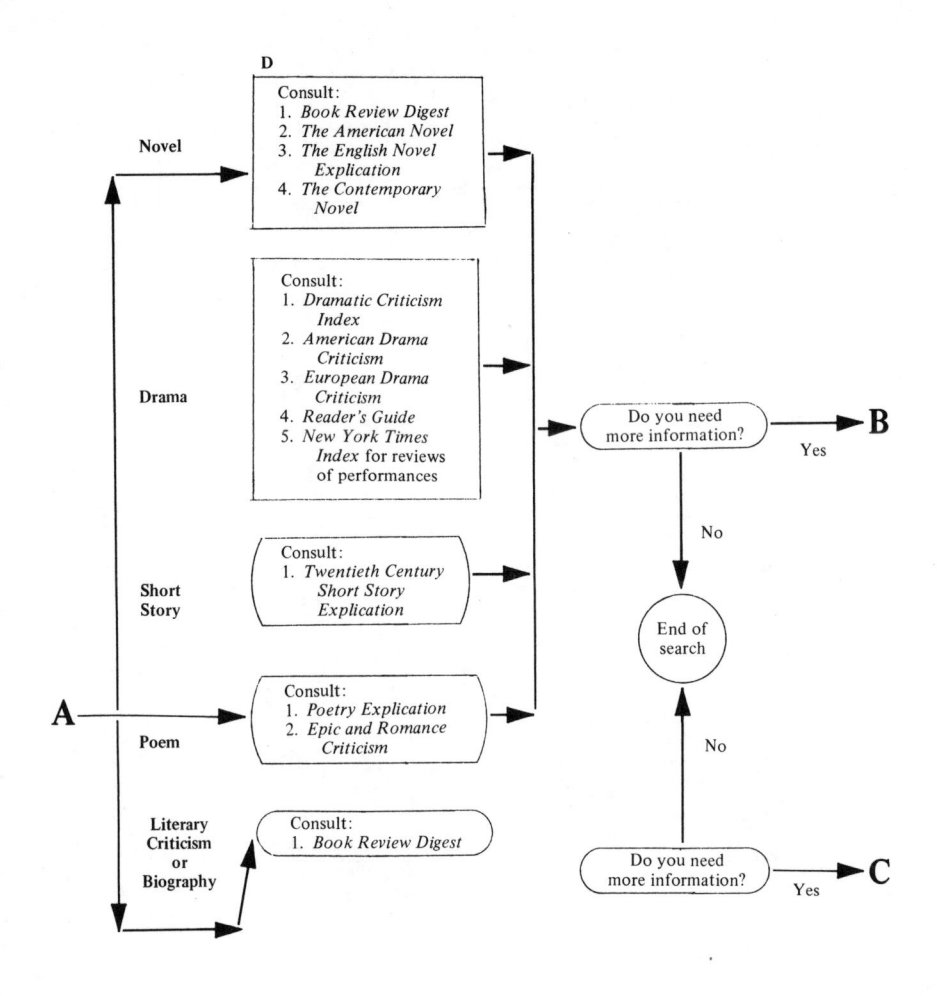

D

Novel → Consult:
1. *Book Review Digest*
2. *The American Novel*
3. *The English Novel Explication*
4. *The Contemporary Novel*

Drama → Consult:
1. *Dramatic Criticism Index*
2. *American Drama Criticism*
3. *European Drama Criticism*
4. *Reader's Guide*
5. *New York Times Index* for reviews of performances

Short Story → Consult:
1. *Twentieth Century Short Story Explication*

A

Poem → Consult:
1. *Poetry Explication*
2. *Epic and Romance Criticism*

Literary Criticism or Biography → Consult:
1. *Book Review Digest*

Do you need more information? — Yes → **B**; No → End of search

Do you need more information? — Yes → **C**; No → End of search

APPENDIX VIII continued –

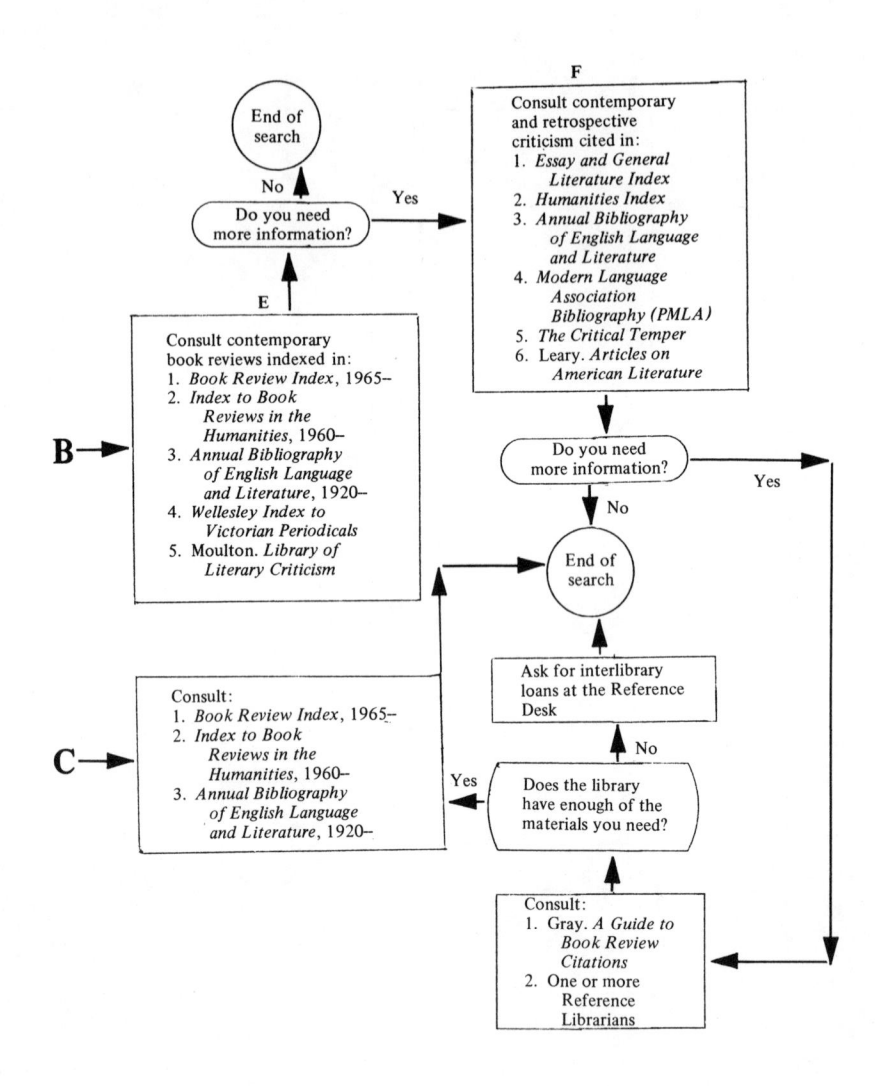

F Consult contemporary and retrospective criticism cited in:
1. *Essay and General Literature Index*
2. *Humanities Index*
3. *Annual Bibliography of English Language and Literature*
4. *Modern Language Association Bibliography (PMLA)*
5. *The Critical Temper*
6. Leary. *Articles on American Literature*

E — **B** → Consult contemporary book reviews indexed in:
1. *Book Review Index*, 1965–
2. *Index to Book Reviews in the Humanities*, 1960–
3. *Annual Bibliography of English Language and Literature*, 1920–
4. *Wellesley Index to Victorian Periodicals*
5. Moulton. *Library of Literary Criticism*

C → Consult:
1. *Book Review Index*, 1965–
2. *Index to Book Reviews in the Humanities*, 1960–
3. *Annual Bibliography of English Language and Literature*, 1920–

Do you need more information? — No → End of search / Yes → (to F)

Do you need more information? — No → End of search / Yes →

Ask for interlibrary loans at the Reference Desk

Does the library have enough of the materials you need? — Yes → (to C box) / No → Ask for interlibrary loans

Consult:
1. Gray. *A Guide to Book Review Citations*
2. One or more Reference Librarians

CRITIQUE OF THE FACULTY DEVELOPMENT AND LIBRARY INSTRUCTION MOVEMENTS: A PANEL DISCUSSION

Sharon J. Rogers

Status differentials certainly exist between teaching faculty and librarians on most campuses in the United States. Traditional academic reward systems, the Ph.D. as the entry–level credential, and the organization and structure of institutions of higher education all operate to create a separate and unequal status for librarians.

One consequence of this status difference is that some of the skills that we are eagerly developing in new definitions of the librarian's role may be viewed as very inappropriate behaviors by our teaching colleagues. For instance, we are learning to ask basic questions about the teaching–learning process in order to explore our interaction with that process. As Patricia Breivik pointed out earlier, we may embarrass our teaching faculty colleagues when we question them about learning objectives, for instance, or the exact purpose of a particular assignment in a course. Therefore, simply asking questions may be construed as threatening behavior and this conflicts with our general image as a low–status, non–threatening group.

Furthermore, the fact that we are asking questions may imply that we are evaluating what is happening in the teaching–learning process. Such a perception challenges the notion Paul Lacey articulated, that librarians are viewed as facilitators, not evaluators, and it adds to our threatening image as we appear to invade the traditional sphere of influence of the teaching faculty.

What kinds of solutions are available to us to deal with such status differentials and the threats that develop when we appear to play our roles in ways that conflict with our status?

Acquisition of the doctoral degree is a solution to part of the problem. However, it will be a long time before the Ph.D/M.L.S. combination appears on library faculties in large enough numbers to allow equal credentialing to modify our image. We need some quicker ways to attack the problem. Since one aspect of the difficulty is the image of librarians as a group, we may need solutions that have a group basis, rather than battling the issue one--on--one in each of our campus arenas.

Let me suggest four ways to neutralize the problem of one--on-one status differences between teaching faculty and librarians. All four of these suggested alternatives will deal with a basic assumption that has been articulated by other speakers: the disciplinary focus is the primary one for most teaching faculty. We need to reach them where they live -- in their disciplines.

First, we need to take our message of new roles for academic librarians to the disciplinary professional associations. Most of the disciplinary professional associations have a section devoted to the improvement of undergraduate teaching in the discipline. For instance, the American Sociological Association has a Project on Undergraduate Teaching funded by the Fund for the Improvement of Post--Secondary Education (FIPSE). The Project sponsors conferences around the country and at national meetings. These disciplinary groups may be very receptive to our exploration of new roles for librarians in the teaching--learning process.

Second, we can work on a professional association to professional association level. The Cooperation Committee of the Bibliographic Instruction Section of ACRL is establishing such contacts and its work needs to be supported.

Third, publishers can be contacted and encouraged to enhance the library image that they project in their disciplinary text materials. Most publishers have at least one title on "how to do a research paper" or "writing the term paper." The section on the library often fails to reflect the complexity of the academic libraries that the target audiences will actually use. We need to let publishers know when their materials do not have maximum usefulness and that our professional expertise is available to assist them.

Fourth, we might examine the instructor's guides that are available with many textbooks. These guides usually contain suggested library exercises or sections on basic literature in a field. They also often contain cursory, even inaccurate information about library resources and how to use libraries. We need to be involved in improving the quality of the information getting to the teaching faculty, and that in turn should help create demand for our services.

John Barber

In this critique, I will express opinions that are based on my involvement in and reading about faculty development, particular--

ly instructional development, during the past two years. My impressions of the library instruction movement derive mainly from a survey of selected literature carried out within the past two months in an effort to compensate for my lack of direct experience. I have found, however, that the latter movement is too vast and complex to grasp very fully in so brief a time, even with the help of Professor Ray Suput, the Director of the Ball State University Library, who provided a large stack of articles. I speak, therefore, as a teacher with some experience in faculty development and as a novice in the library instruction movement. But, above all, you should consider my remarks to be those of a faculty member who is deeply concerned about and committed to the goals of both movements as he presently conceives them.

My concern and commitment indicate that, in a sense, I am beginning my presentation with an implied critique of higher education, for I am suggesting that we need the advance in faculty quality and the progress in student bibliographic skills that these two relatively new movements are trying to encourage. I agree with Dwight Burlingame who used a Victor Hugo quotation to emphasize the view that faculty development and library instruction are ideas whose time has come. On our campus, for example, as several of the conference participants know from experience in related activities, a program called the Project on Institutional Renewal through the Improvement of Teaching is under way. Professor Jerry Gaff, who directs this multi-state effort, his staff, and the project teams on this and about twenty other campuses, are helping to build a valuable instructional development program within the larger structure of faculty development here at Ball State. I have been much impressed by, and in many positive ways affected by, "Project Renewal." Remarks by other speakers indicate that the work directed by Professor Gaff has also influenced their thoughts and activities. These are signs that a new stimulus to professional faculty growth has come at a time when, to me, it seems esepcially necessary.

On our campus also faculty and staff members have begun a project, supported by the National Endowment for the Humanities, which will lead to the establishment of a library instruction program. Since the English and History Departments are involved in the first stage of this movement, I have had an opportunity to see the potential benefits that should come in the very near future. I would like to see this project thrive as have other library instruction programs about which I have read. I hope for this success because there is now a more urgent need than ever for professors and students to learn how to use bibliographic resources.

What I have observed at Ball State, what I have learned through the literature on faculty development and library instruction, and what I have heard in this conference today indicates, therefore, that these movements are very much alive. That is good. What bothers me, however, is that they were so late in coming. I believe they came almost at the end of the time when we could continue a really viable higher education program without the influence of such movements. In my less optimistic moments, I wonder if this new drive for faculty growth and advance in student bibliographic skills did not begin too late. This possibility really troubles me on occasion. My fears arise in part because the last current to emerge in the faculty development movement was the concern for instruction, which I think is the most vital element. And the library instruction movement came to life still later, despite the possibility that its effects were more needed than those of the instructional development movement. So, I am pleased to see these efforts under way but displeased that they have only begun.

I would like to make another point on the positive side in my critique of these movements. Through my experiences in faculty development, I have found that many people involved in these programs have the qualities necessary to ensure success in a very late hour. The trait that I especially value is their enthusiasm. I believe that among certain participants in faculty development and among academic librarians whom I have observed here, this spirit of enthusiasm is constructive because it appears to grow from a common sense of deep-seated social and learning needs that now affect large numbers of people. I see it as positive also because it stems, I believe, from their caring about these people. This enthusiasm, comprised of a certain energy and vision, indicates a recognition of the real nature of the problems in the world around us and shows a deep sense of the importance of striving for solutions. When the speeches and conversations that I hear among people in these movements reveal that they too have the fears that I have but also the hopes and goals that I have, that sense of a shared concern and common enterprise induces a beneficial enthusiasm. It does so especially when the professional attitudes one values are seen to exist beyond one's own campus.

Another quality that I have noticed among many people in these movements is that they are experts who know how to provide valuable services. The academic librarians at Ball State have impressed me very much in this respect. They not only respond effectively and efficiently to my requests; they also call or use chance encounters to ask, "Could you use this?" "Would it help you if we did that?" And if I accept an offer for assistance, they deliver expertly. The staff of the Ball State Office of Research, small as it is, and overworked as it is, amazes me with its effectiveness in helping professors whose direction of development touches their area. The work of the people in this branch of the faculty development program, as well as the performance of our academic librarians, suggests that the two movements on which this conference has focused attention have or can draw on participants who possess a very useful expert knowledge. This is a quality that we need in order to ensure the success of these efforts.

I am pleased, therefore, about much that I see in these movements. But I want to impress you more deeply with my thoughts on features that displease me. In stating this intention, I do not mean to imply that the flaws are greater than the strengths. I want to emphasize problems in the movements in part because I take the word "critique" to mean an assessment that concentrates on flaws. But the more important reason for underscoring weaknesses is that a critique, above all, should point out errors that might need correction.

In the first place, I think that both movements have done far too little to learn about the current personal and social needs of the billions of people who inhabit this world. I noted above that the enthusiasm of certain participants arises from this kind of social insight. But too few people in these movements have this awareness. When we have shaped our faculty development and library instruction programs, we have done so far too often without taking a hard look at the traits of the people we are to serve. And we also have paid too little attention to our own human qualities and needs. We have not sufficiently informed our efforts with knowledge of what it means to be human.

If I am a faculty member, I am nevertheless also a person with many needs that exist just because I am human. And when people deal with librarians, they too often think of and respond to them as stereotypes rather than as real people, as one commentator noted this morning. The problem for students is even greater. We deal with each other as objects, and we relate to students in an even more insensitive way. The people with whom we work too frequently become things to be manipulated, and we treat them that way because "that's the way it has been done."

I have a great respect for tradition. I want tradition to guide us in the faculty development and library instruction movements. But I think that we must realize what we are like . . . right now . . . as humans. And we must see where humanity is going and become fully aware of emerging needs. As we continue these movements in the future, we should do so with a full consciousness of human qualities and needs. We must know our weaknesses and strengths. We must understand the emotional and intellectual make up of humans.

Except for those in the life sciences, faculty members who have made any effort to learn about how the brain works surely are rare. Show me one from another field who is well informed in this respect and I will applaud him or her. I believe that faculty members or librarians who try to understand cognition and cognitive development are equally rare. And who among us has made a sufficient effort to perceive the social problems of our age and their implications for our work? Above all, I would argue that we have not begun to shape the faculty development and library instruction movements according to the traits of the people we are to serve, and in light of the problems with which their world confronts them. We have not met the students, librarians, and teachers where they are. We have acted with too little awareness of the ignorance and weakness that afflicts us all and with an inadequate sense of the knowledge and power that equips us all. In short, we have not yet done enough to use these movements to help people learn what they must in order to thrive under current conditions. Until we learn more about human traits and needs and inform these movements with our discoveries, we help to ensure that humanity moves blindly at a time when we can not afford this risk.

My criticism implies that those of us in these movements lack an adequate sense of the meaning of our work. We lack a clear understanding of what our living and our professions are about. This absence of meaning or clarity is reflected in much of what we say and write. Read the literature on library instruction. Read the articles and books on faculty development. Read item after item on almost any academic subject. If you do so and are not irritated by the jargon that hides muddled thought and prevents clear communication, then your mind must be elsewhere than on your reading. Perhaps I should not be bothered to hear and read the superfluous expression "in terms of" which is so constantly repeated along with many other academic cliches; but I am bothered. Yet I single out none of you for criticism for what troubles me. I am criticizing myself and most of us in higher education because our communication is too often jargon-filled, and because I think that this means we do not know enough about what we are doing. Thus when we try to speak or write, we fill too much time and space with words and phrases that are meaningless.

Jargon, therefore, is a second fundamental problem that I see in the faculty development and library instruction movements. It is an almost unavoidable corollary of the larger problem that I discussed earlier in this critique -- our inadequate grasp of human traits and needs and the failure to guide higher education with the necessary insight into ourselves. How can we develop properly as faculty members, and how can we teach students how to use sources in the library to their best advantage, if we do not know what our living is all about, and if we do not know how to communicate clearly?

I am deeply thankful that today I have heard people say things that were meaningful, and that they said them clearly. I am encouraged by this experience, as I almost always am at such conferences. The events of the day strengthen my belief that a sense of meaning and skill in communication will affect the faculty development and library instruction movements in the future. And I have to believe that, or else I would quit.

George L. Gardiner

No other single institutional resource, I believe, should have a more positive, long--term impact on the educational progress and intellectual growth of the students than the university library. This should result from several collaborative efforts including the interaction of students and faculty with library collections, policies, and services as well as the response of the library to the needs articulated by students and faculty. The faculty's role is crucial. In conjunction with its advancement in teaching and scholarship, the faculty must make a considerable contribution to the library as a learning resource through its involvement in the building of library collections, the development of library policies and services, and the guidance of students in the use of the library.

Within the framework of this belief and as a member of the Provost's Personnel Committee at Oakland University, a committee which has responsibility for making general policy and specific judgments in recommendations to the Provost on all matters and cases relating to faculty appointment, re--employment, tenure and promotion, I attempt to play a facilitative role in the joint development of the library and of the faculty by raising the following questions on re--employment and tenure cases: What has the candidate contributed to the library as an institutional resource? In what ways and how well has the candidate integrated the resource of the library into the teaching process? (I may, on occasion and as appropriate, substitute the computing center or the learning skills laboratory for the library.) I hope, in the words of Professor Lacey, that I have framed important questions in raising these issues. They are by no means the only questions I raise but they are the most important questions I raise as dean of the library. Indeed, I should like to raise additional questions about the faculty's contribution to the library and the learning process through the questionnaires commonly distributed among students and used to evaluate the faculty member's teaching performance: Did the instructor assist you in learning and mastering the bibliographic tools underlying the discipline? Did the instructor encourage you to read in depth and independently in the subject matter of the course? I believe that Oakland cannot be a quality institution with a strong faculty and a strong library unless the faculty makes a significant contribution to the library and the faculty understands that it should do so.

Several years ago we made a purposeful decision at Oakland to raise standards in the several criteria under which faculty are reviewed for tenure, namely, in teaching or primary job responsibilities among librarians, scholarship and service, as opposed to instituting tenure quotas. Current evidence indicates the wisdom of that decision. Junior members of the faculty have risen to the challenge of more rigorous standards. Indeed, they are raising standards. They may be characterized as self-developing. As John D. Millett noted several years ago, self-development is a choice that a faculty member makes for himself:

> Perhaps no profession – not even law or medicine – leaves so much determination of effort entirely in the hands of the faculty member himself . . . . How hard the faculty member works at his field of specialization, whether he gives primary attention to teaching or to research, how and what he desires to write and publish, how much he reads, how much he participates in professional activity and association, how rapidly he seeks to advance himself professionally – these are largely decisions the faculty member makes for himself . . . by and large the faculty member determines his own career.[1]

A necessary condition for self-development among librarians as well as teaching faculty is the existence of high-performance standards and, therefore, I would urge librarians to institute standards, where they do not exist, or to raise the standards of their professional performance, scholarship and service which prevail in matters of initial appointment, continued appointment and, where applicable, tenure or job security in academic libraries.

Too many -- by no means the majority – of the senior faculty at Oakland, on the other hand, are not rising to the challenge of more rigorous standards. Some seem filled with resentment, perhaps fear, but, most obviously, with unyielding resistance to this among the many changes which have and are occurring in the world in which we live. A few have completely withdrawn from the academic life.

In one area the majority of the faculty is adamant in its refusal to change. That is in its attitude as to what constitutes the academy. If I understood Professors McCartney and Lacey correctly this morning, they, among others, still believe the faculty to be the academy and the academy to be the faculty. All others, administrators, board members, clerical staff, librarians, and students are, in a personal sense, subservient to this group. Peter F. Drucker expresses this attitude as clearly as anyone:

> A library is above all a continuous attempt to impose a little order on chaos. Information is basically chaotic, and in order to make it useable you have to have some order, and that requires a great deal of donkey work. In addition, all users leave disorder in their wake because they are not concerned with costs but only with their own needs . . . . No matter what you do, your users, whether they are your best faculty or students, leave chaos in their wake, and you run after them the way the fellow in the circus runs after the elephant with the dustpan.[2]

I do not believe, as asserted this morning, that librarians have an essential role in assisting the faculty by keeping overhead projectors in repair or evidencing sympathy for the faculty member's stress or enhancing the faculty's satisfaction in teaching or trailing behind the faculty with a dustpan. Librarians do have an essential role in collaborating in the teaching–learning process, in enhancing the environment of learning and scholarship, in assisting the entire campus community in the pursuit of academic excellence.

Although Mr. Burlingame has become bored with the issue of the image of librarians, I must beg his and your indulgence just once more on this matter. In an article in the *Library Quarterly* several years ago, Ralph Edwards suggested that as a consequence of working in bureaucratic environments, librarians suffer from low self and institutional images.[3] In Edwards' view, executive authority permeates the hierarchical form of organization to the extent that librarians serving within such settings can neither behave nor be perceived as professional persons. A second condition necessary for the self–development of librarians is their freedom from excessively bureaucratic kinds of organization and their acceptance of the consequences and responsibilities of self–determination in their job roles.

The majority of us who are assembled here today are vitally concerned with library instruction as a vehicle through which librarians are making important contributions to the teaching–learning process. While library instruction represents one of the most significant statements which librarians have made in recent years in terms of their self-development, progress has not come easily and much progress lies ahead. In some institutions library instruction has been the concern of a single librarian who, upon leaving the institution, took with him or herself the library's instructional program. In some institutions, library instruction has been instituted for the wrong reasons. For example, some librarians have become frustrated with the routines of reference desk service or believed that some form of teaching would assist them in gaining faculty status. In some instances, library instruction has not been given administrative support within the library and, consequently, has had to be conducted underground if not clandestinely. To the extent that academic libraries and librarians continue to pursue instruction as a viable service program, I hope that they will do it not only in the formal framework of a program document with well formulated goals and objectives as well as a committee or task force given the responsibility of policy making, information exchange and program evaluation, but also that they will do it within an institutionalized framework. A formal program is sufficient to institutionalize instruction within the library; to be institutionalized within the parent college or university, it should not only be recognized by professional associations, as Professor Rogers has mentioned, and by accrediting associations, as I would suggest to Professor Rogers, but should be institutionalized in the sense of being adequately described in the institution's one or several student catalogs. Library instruction also deserves professional institutionalization within the framework of graduate library education. To this end, I urge greater development and support of instruction by the graduate library schools perhaps beginning with the nature and import of bibliographic instruction but expanding into the nature and import of library and information instruction.

Some librarians think and work within the framework of the limited objectives of the specific department in which they are employed; others, within the framework of the specific library in which they work; some few think and work within the framework of each of these levels but also within the framework of educational ideals as well as the goals and objectives of the institutions which they serve. Those who think and work in the impoverished areas of this scale can have no vision of what they or the profession can become. A third condition necessary for the self-development of librarians is the need for present and future visions. Let me try to illustrate a single aspect of my meaning with a somewhat artificial example. Chairing Harvard's undergraduate curriculum review committee, Dean Henry Rosovsky has outlined five characteristics which can be expected of an educated person in the twentieth century:

(1) To think and communicate clearly and effectively
(2) to have a critical appreciation of how physical and social knowledge is gained
(3) to develop an understanding of other cultures and other times
(4) to be able to make reasoned ethical and moral decisions
(5) to achieve depth in a field of knowledge.[4]

To the extent that these characteristics represent educational goals which can be translated into innovative programs, librarians not only have a right but a responsibility to ask themselves how we can, with our unique competencies, experiences and methodologies, assist our institutions in developing these characteristics among the students we serve.

Speaking in Detroit this past spring Alphonse F. Trezza, the executive director of the National Commission on Libraries and Information Science, invited all librarians to join him and others in participating in the advances occurring and about to occur in librarianship but suggested that those who had no vision for the future likewise had no commitments to the present, that those who were satisfied with the status quo and were unprepared to move ahead would be passed over by the profession.[5] Involvement in faculty development programs, except as co--equal partners, does not represent progress for academic librarians. As a group and as individuals I urge librarians to be concerned with their own self--development and progress: to be concerned with raising the standards against which their performance is evaluated, to be concerned with improving their role and image in the academic community, to be concerned with the institutionalizing of library instruction programs, to be concerned with their vision of academic library services. Academic librarians, like faculty, enjoy considerable flexibility in determining their personal advancement and the advancement of the profession. Each day of our professional lives each of us enjoys the opportunity to choose the status quo or to choose something new, untried, something which may seem a little out of reach.

FOOTNOTES

1. Millet, John D. *An Essay on Organization: the Academic Community*. (New York: McGraw--Hill, 1962), pp. 68-69.

2. Drucker, Peter F. "Managing the Public Service Institution" *College & Research Libraries*, 37 (January 1976), p. 12.

3. Edwards, Ralph M. "The Management of Libraries and the Professional Functions of Librarians" *Library Quarterly*, 45 (April 1975), pp. 156–57.

4. See "Harvard Weighs Plan to Reform College Curriculum," *Chronicle of Higher Education*, 16 (March 6, 1978), p. 15.

5. Trezza, Alphonse F. "Libraries 1978: Goals for Action," speech presented at the Alumni Update program, Wayne State University, Division of Library Science, May 6, 1978.

Marilyn D. Ward

What is faculty development? There are numerous definitions of faculty development that have been offered by the experts. Berquist and Phillips[1] describe three components of faculty development: 1. instructional development, 2. organizational development, and 3. personal development. Gaff[2] defines faculty development as only one of three areas of a total instructional improvement program which includes organizational development and instructional improvement as the other two components. Webb and Smith[3] offer four models of faculty development that are supported either in practice or theory. The first of these is the scholarship model, which is based on the assumption that the better the scholar, the better the teacher. Programs using this model are designed to provide faculty with opportunities for research usually in the form of a sabbatical or released time. The second approach to improving instruction is a model that emphasizes instructional development. Based on a probelm–solving approach, the professional staff of a center work with individual faculty to create a more effective instructional system. The third model, developed by Fraley and Vargas,[4] is that of changing the faculty role. This model is largely a theoretical model because of the tremendous resources required and the difficulty of implementation. The fourth model is one of organization and personal growth which assumes that any attempt at instructional improvement must be focused on the individual faculty members and the environment in which they work. The programs using this model usually emphasize two areas. The first is that of changing the institution itself for the purpose of providing faculty with an environment that is conducive to the professional and personal growth of the individual. The second emphasis is on the individual faculty member and consists of a wide variety of activities ranging from improving specific teaching behaviors to career counseling.

All of these models and definitions of faculty development have one common goal and that is improvement of teaching. According to Gaff,[5] instructional behavior of faculty members is a learned complex of knowledge, attitudes, values, motivations, skills and sensitivities, and he indicates that faculty members may learn to improve these instructional competencies.

One of the first steps to take in order to help improve these competencies of faculty members is to help them change their own perception of their role as a subject-matter specialist to that of a teacher or facilitatior of learning. If one were to query professors about their profession most would respond by proclaiming themselves to be historians, psychologists, chemists, etc. rather than teachers.

Another step that must be taken is that of informing the faculty about the wealth of material available concerning research in teaching improvement and instructional design. On most campuses librarians prepare bibliographies from different disciplines but have not generally sent out bibliographies or materials available that deal with teaching methods and materials. Many faculty are not aware of the abundance of articles and books that are currently being published in the area of instructional science. Centra[6] lists as one of the twelve important and useful faculty development practices that of special, professional libraries readily accessible to faculty, dealing with instructional methodology, teaching and similar topics. Linquist[7] lists as one of his ten strategies for improving college teaching the dissemination of teaching and learning theory. Librarians are charged with the acquisiton and publicizing of such a collection.

Also needed is a place for faculty to get together to exchange ideas about teaching. The library is the logical place for such a purpose and as librarians perhaps the most important service you could provide would be the creation of such an area. This area would contain books, and journals concerned with improvement of teaching and instructional science.

There are a lot of things remaining to be done in faculty development. Gaff[8] says that the organizational structure you provide for faculty is important, that you bring together the media center, the computer center, the library and an instructional improvement center and you make these services truly useful to the faculty. He also points out, however, that it takes a great deal of effort to get these things working together, that simply putting them together on an organizational chart does not always accomplish the things you need.

There is much being done in the area of faculty development but there is more to do and librarians can not only help but are necessary because if they are the source of information about teaching improvement they will aid in legitimizing faculty development in the eyes of the faculty.

FOOTNOTES

1. Berquist, W. H., and Phillips, S. R., "Components of an Effective Faculty Development Program," *Journal of Higher Education*, 46 (1975), 177–211.

2. Gaff, J. G., *Toward Faculty Renewal*, San Francisco: Jossey–Bass, 1975.

3. Webb, J. N., and Smith, A. B., "Improving Instruction in Higher Education", *Educational Horizons*, 1977, 86–91.

4. Fraley, L. E., and Vargas, E. A., "Academic Tradition and Instructional Technology", *Journal of Higher Education*, 46 (1975), 1–15.

5. Gaff, J. G. *op cit.*

6. Centra, J. A., *Faculty Development Practices in U.S. Colleges and Universities*, PR–76–30. Princeton, N.J.: Educational Testing Service, 1976.

7. Linquist, J., *Designing Teaching Improvement Programs*, Berkley, California: Pacific Soundings Press, 1978.

8. Gaff, J. G., "Current Issues in Faculty Development", *Liberal Education*, 63 (1977), 511–519.

LIBRARY INSTRUCTION -- THE BEST ROAD TO DEVELOPMENT FOR FACULTY, LIBRARIANS AND STUDENTS

William K. Stephenson

There is a trinity of persons who are involved in the development of institutional programs of library instruction -- faculty, librarians, and students. Faculty members are the most obstreperous component of this triad.

What are faculty persons really like? I suggest three characteristics relevant to this discussion; faculty members are disciplinary chauvinists, they want to be good teachers, and they are insecure.

All librarians know that college faculty persons are disciplinary chauvinists. We faculty don't want to give up the time our students spend on subject matter for training in literature accessing skills. We don't want to learn from librarians. We feel that the most effective learning is learning in our narrow subject matter disciplines. I don't want to give up time in biology for "less important things." As librarians you need to recognize this disciplinary chauvinism, and you need to use it in working with your faculty to gain their support and involvement.

Preceding articles have shown the value of incorporating library instructions into the educational progams of an institution -- how this can contribute to the development of individual faculty and can increase the ability of students to learn within academic disciplines. I also suggest that a faculty member will be a better subject matter specialist if she or he integrates training in the accessing of literature into course work. Faculty members need what librarians have to offer. As a faculty person who has used library instruction for almost a decade, I know this. The problem is that most faculty members don't yet know that they need librarians. Since faculty members are disciplinary chauvinists, we need librarians to help us to grow beyond that chauvinism by leading us to utilize library instruction.

Librarians know that good teaching must involve library training. Faculty members want to be good teachers. Most of us faculty, however, lack the training in library skills, accessing, and developing search strategies. Overall, we lack the training for effectively incorporating library training into our academic courses and into our departmental programs. I know this from my own experience.

Consider the first year that we used library instruction in our department. After two quarters of training, my students were more skilled at literature access than I was. That led me to feel even more insecure about library learning than usual.

Faculty members *are* insecure in at least two major dimensions. We are insecure as scholars. As teachers, we are expected to know everything in our fields, and of course we fall short in this. Therefore we are defensive about being challenged on points of knowledge and authority in our subject matter specialties.

Faculty members are also insecure as teachers. Most faculty have personal histories of having been good students. Through grade school, junior high, and high school, we were the achievers. We earned good grades, awards, and the honors of academic achievement. We have been evaluated highly as scholars, and we are not accustomed to receiving low marks. It is ironic that as teachers we evaluate with confidence and impunity, even arrogance, but we don't want to be evaluated as teachers. Most of us are threatened by student evaluation. When the student evaluation forms and summary sheets are returned, even the best teachers that I know open that envelope with trepidation. Teachers of modest ability by their own admission, open the envelope with "terror in their hearts."

Library educators must be sensitive to these insecurities in their own faculty members. They need to be sensitive to them and still have the maturity to put up with overbearing academic-intellectual egos and with the attitudes of superiority that most individual faculty members exhibit. I know this is difficult, but to be effective it is essential that librarians tolerate the disciplinary chauvinism and the façade of super-competence that faculty persons attempt to present.

The development of librarians has also been stressed in this symposium. Librarians must develop their personal abilities in an atmosphere of rapid changes, especially changes in technology and in the role of libraries in higher education. I think that there are also three effective areas in which librarians should attempt to effect personal changes: leadership, assertiveness, and enthusiasm.

The role of librarians is changing from passive to cooperative -- with faculty as coworkers in the educational enterprise. I think that the librarian's role must change further to involve increasing leadership in undergraduate and graduate education. Librarians occupy positions and perform functions that are increasingly central to higher education. A caricature that many people have of the librarian is a rather passive individual. For the college librarians of my experience this is an inaccurate stereotype. Inaccurate though it may be, librarians themselves must become more assertive in order to deliver the leadership that is essential for the extension and success of library education programs. Faculty members are very aggressive within the academic–intellectual milieu of the university. To be effective, librarians must be able to match the level of assertiveness of faculty. Overall, the development of library instruction must shift from being a passive process, waiting to be consulted, to an active process.

Librarians also need to develop and to project a greater level of enthusiasm about their work. In my judgment, the single most important factor in good teaching is enthusiasm. The effective teacher projects enthusiasm about the subject matter and instills students with enthusiasm for the material. Librarians are showing increasing enthusiasm for library instruction. This is an essential aspect of your development as teachers, and it will be necessary to project that enthusiasm to your faculty colleagues and to students who are undertaking library instruction.

The forgotten member of the original triad are the students. Successful students also need to develop three effective qualities that relate to learning – enthusiasm, self–confidence, and independence.

Students should develop an enthusiasm for life–long learning. One cannot motivate students about things they are not involved with, or interested in. This means that library instruction should be conducted in the context of subject matter courses and departmental programs. Ideally, library instruction should *not* be accomplished by orientation tours, in single lectures on library use, or in specialized library–skills courses. Student enthusiasm for learning is most often associated with departmental programs, individual courses, and subject matter content.

Students also need to develop self–confidence in learning that is based upon confidence in their ability to use the library. One of the goals in our departmental program of library instruction in biology at Earlham College is that ten years hence students should be able to locate and evaluate information on any scientific topic. We are attempting to design a library instruction program that will develop the competence and self–confidence that will support a life–long learning process. This necessitates repeated practice in literature search. One doesn't develop confidence and competence by reading about library techniques or by participating in a single trial.

Mature students should also be able to locate information independently; they should be able to function independent of faculty, the subject matter experts, and independent of librarians, the information retrieval experts. An effective program of library instruction should train students toward that goal of independent scholarship.

Librarians occupy an enviable position in higher education because they are part of one of the most rapidly developing com--ponents of the educational process. There is an expanding need for library instruction. Library instruction programs are enjoying increasing accomplishment and recognition. Librarians are being challenged to develop not only in the cognitive areas of subject matter, search capabilities, technology, and skills, but also in the affective areas of enthusiasm, assertiveness, and leadership. If librarians can meet this challenge of their own personal and profes--sional development successfully, they can be of tremendous value to the development of students and to the development of faculty colleagues.

CONTRIBUTORS

Barber, Dr. John. Associate Professor of History, Ball State University. Member of University Directive Team for Project on Institutional Renewal Through the Improvement of Teaching, 1976-78. Member of Advisory Council of Ball State University Office of Instructional Development.

Breivik, Dr. Patricia Senn. Director, Auraria Libraries, University of Colorado at Denver. Formerly Dean of Library Services, Sangamon State University.

Burlingame, Dr. Dwight F. Dean of Libraries and Learning Resources, Bowling Green State University. Formerly Dean of Learning Resources at University of Evansville.

Farber, Evan Ira. Librarian, Earlham College. Consultant and author of several articles and books on library instruction. President of Association of College and Research Libraries, 1978-79.

Gardiner, George L. Dean of the Library, Oakland University. Formerly Director of the Library, Central State University at Wilberforce.

Lacey, Dr. Paul A. Professor of English, Earlham College. Formerly Provost of Earlham College. Worked with Faculty development at Earlham and in Great Lakes Colleges Association. Currently Faculty Consultant on Teaching and Learning at Earlham.

McCartney, Dr. Jesse. Director, Office of Instructional Development, Ball State University. Formerly Associate Professor of English at University of Southern Mississippi.

Rogers, Dr. Sharon J. Social Science Subject Specialist for University Libraries, University of Toledo.

Stephenson, Dr. William K. Professor of Biology, Earlham College.

Ward, Marilyn D. Director, Curriculum Laboratory and Assistant Professor of Learning Resources, Western Illinois University.

Suput, Dr. Ray R. Univeristy Librarian and Professor of Library Service. Formerly Assistant Director of University Libraries and Lecturer in Slavic Linguistics and Library Science, Case Western

Reserve University.

Tsukamoto, Dr. Jack T. Associate Professor of Library Service and Head of Division of Processing, Ball State University. Formerly Assistant Professor of Japanese and Linguistics, Washington University in St. Louis.

Williams, Dr. Nyal Z. Associate Professor of Library Service and Music Librarian, Ball State University. Formerly Assistant Music Librarian, University of North Carolina at Chapel Hill.

LIBRARY ORIENTATION SERIES

Number one: LIBRARY ORIENTATION; Papers Presented at the First Annual Conference on Library Orientation held at Eastern Michigan University, May 7, 1971.

Number two: A CHALLENGE FOR ACADEMIC LIBRARIES: HOW TO MOTIVATE STUDENTS TO USE THE LIBRARY; Papers Presented at the Second Annual Conference on Library Orientation for Academic Libraries, Eastern Michigan University, May 4-5, 1972.

Number three: PLANNING AND DEVELOPING A LIBRARY ORIENTATION PROGRAM; Proceedings of the Third Annual Conference on Library Orientation for Academic Libraries, Eastern Michigan University, May 3-4, 1973.

Number four: EVALUATING LIBRARY USE INSTRUCTION; Papers Presented at the University of Denver Conference on the Evaluation of Library Use Instruction, December 13-14, 1973.

Number five: ACADEMIC LIBRARY INSTRUCTION: OBJECTIVES, PROGRAMS, AND FACULTY INVOLVEMENT; Papers of the Fourth Annual Conference on Library Orientation for Academic Libraries, Eastern Michigan University, May 9-11, 1974.

Number six: FACULTY INVOLVEMENT IN LIBRARY INSTRUCTION: THEIR VIEWS ON PARTICIPATION IN AND SUPPORT OF ACADEMIC LIBRARY USE INSTRUCTION; Papers and Summaries from the Fifth Annual Conference on Library Orientation for Academic Libraries held at Eastern Michigan University, May 15-17, 1975.

Number seven: LIBRARY INSTRUCTION IN THE SEVENTIES: STATE OF THE ART; Papers Presented at the Sixth Annual Conference on Library Orientation for Academic Libraries held at Eastern Michigan University, May 13-14, 1976.

Number eight: PUTTING LIBRARY INSTRUCTION IN ITS PLACE: IN THE LIBRARY AND IN THE LIBRARY SCHOOL; Papers Presented at the Seventh Annual Conference on Library Orientation for Academic Libraries held at Eastern Michigan University, May 12-13, 1977.

Number nine: IMPROVING LIBRARY INSTRUCTION: HOW TO TEACH AND HOW TO EVALUATE; Papers Presented at the Eighth Annual Conference on Library Orientation for Academic Libraries held at Eastern Michigan University, May 4-5, 1978.

Number ten: REFORM AND RENEWAL IN HIGHER EDUCATION: IMPLICATIONS FOR LIBRARY INSTRUCTION; Papers Presented at the Ninth Annual Conference on Library Orientation for Academic Libraries held at Eastern Michigan University, May 3-4, 1979.

Number eleven: LIBRARY INSTRUCTION AND FACULTY DEVELOPMENT: GROWTH OPPORTUNITIES IN THE ACADEMIC COMMUNITY; Papers Presented at the Twenty-Third Midwest Academic Librarians' Conference held at Ball State University, May 1978.

LIBRARY INSTRUCTION AND FACULTY DEVELOPMENT